THE CHARACTER OF GOD

THE CHARACTER OF GOD

DAVID PAWSON

ANCHOR RECORDINGS

First published in Great Britain in 2014 by
Anchor Recordings Ltd
72 The Street
Kennington, Ashford TN24 9HS

**For more of David Pawson's teaching,
including MP3s, DVDs and CDs, go to
www.davidpawson.com
For further information,
email info@davidpawsonministry.com**

ISBN 978-1-909886-34-6

Printed by Lightning Source

Contents

This book is based on a series of talks. Originating as it does from the spoken word, its style will be found by many readers to be somewhat different from my usual written style. It is hoped that this will not detract from the substance of the biblical teaching found here.

As always, I ask the reader to compare everything I say or write with what is written in the Bible and, if at any point a conflict is found, always to rely upon the clear teaching of scripture.

David Pawson

1

ALMIGHTY, BOUNTIFUL CREATOR

"Have you not known? Have you not heard? The Lord is the everlasting God, the Creator of the ends of the earth" (Isaiah 40:28). It is as if the prophet is saying: if you don't know this, where have you been?

This short book is about God, and I want to try to keep it very simple. It is meant to help those who have difficulty believing in him. I want you to feel that he is real and that he wants you to know him personally, and that he is able to help you.

If I said to a child, "God made you" then sooner or later the child would come up with this real stickler of a question: "Well then, who made God?" But you are an adult, and you wouldn't ask a question like that, would you? There is in fact a very simple answer. But, first of all, I am concerned with the fact that **God made you**.

In what I write about God, I have no intention of impugning any reader's intelligence, but I am going to use the alphabet as an aid to memory. We will take the first three letters of the alphabet: A, B, C. We begin with the *A*lmighty, *B*ountiful *C*reator—that is where Christian belief begins. Christians who use creeds in their churches usually begin by saying this: "I believe in God, the Father Almighty, Maker of heaven and earth...." It's the "Maker" part that we are going to begin with.

How do I know that God is the Creator? What makes me believe that? I know it because God has told me in three different ways that he is the Creator. First, he has told me through the things that he has made and, second, he has told me through the Bible. I will keep the third a secret until we get there.

First, then, God has told me that he is the Creator through the things that he has created.

If you ever go to St. Paul's Cathedral you will find in one little corner a tablet telling you about Sir Christopher Wren who built that wonderful building. Roughly translated from Latin, it says, "If you seek his monument, look around you." You see that there isn't one monument to him, just the things that he planned, things he brought into being after the Great Fire of London had destroyed so many churches. If you seek God's monument, look around and it exists. Sir Christopher Wren is long since dead and gone, but God is alive. If you seek *his* living monument, look around you. A poet wrote: "Every common bush is aflame with God. There are those who sit around and pluck blackberries and miss the whole show."

Many years ago I visited the little village of Kilburn, North Yorkshire. In a little shed there a man called "Thompson", a real craftsman in wood, did his work. They called him "Mousey Thompson" because he never carved a thing without inscribing a little mouse somewhere on it. Since those days, if I have gone into a church and noticed some woodwork has been done, I have often looked around for a mouse and been able to find it. Then I have said, "I recognise the work of the maker of that. I can see a 'stamp' of the maker. Mousey Thompson did that." Even though you have not met Mousey Thompson yourself, I think you would be inclined to accept my word for it that I recognised his handiwork.

Again and again in the Psalms you find that David recognises the work of the Maker. "When I look at the heavens, the work of thy fingers..." says the psalmist. If you can look up at a starry sky and not think of God, there is something seriously wrong. The stars are the work of his fingers; he created each one of them. Or, again applying to the stars, Psalm 19, "The heavens are telling the glory of God and the firmament showeth..." What? The handiwork of God, the Creator.

It has led many people who don't know him to call him "the great architect of the universe" and other similar terms. There is a much better name for God.

Let us look at this from three points of view. First of all: *the existence of anything at all*. To ask me to believe that all this that we see around us just happened, that it came into being of itself, is asking me to believe something far harder than my asking someone to believe that someone made it. A little poem comes to mind:

> "There is no God," the speaker cries,
> "Don't let your thoughts be chained.
> The universe evolved itself.
> The world is self-contained."
> Just then an urchin in the crowd
> a skilful pebble throws,
> which accurately lands upon
> his atheistic nose.
> "Who threw that stone?" the speaker roars.
> At which the cockney elf, intuitively keen, retorts,
> "No one! It frew itself."

You ask me to be an atheist and I say you are asking me to have more faith than if you asked me to believe in the Creator. The very fact that things exist! It seems incredible that all this just happened by itself. As one philosopher put it, "It's as if you asked me to believe that an infinite number of monkeys, playing with an infinite number of typewriters, could sooner or later produce the complete works of Shakespeare."

It is just asking too much of us, and there is not only the matter of *existence* but the *design*. I thank God that I had the privilege of studying science before becoming a minister. I remember one day I spent the afternoon in a laboratory with a microscope, and I spent the evening lying in the cradle of a large telescope at Cambridge University Observatory. Those two experiences together filled me with a sense of awe and wonder. I was so thankful I was a believer. To be able to look through those lenses and in both cases see the most amazing design! I remember the thrill with which I discovered that a blade of grass is more complex than the mechanism which is my car. You ask me to believe that there is no Creator? Yet there is a further point. The firm that produced my car manages to produce a new model every three years, but there are thousands of cars like mine. But I remember the day that I realised there are no two identical blades of grass in the whole universe. Man's originality and inventiveness can't produce more than one new model every three years, yet God in his bountiful variety has so created the world that as I drive along I don't see two trees alike. "Poems are made by fools like me," said a preacher, "but only God can make a tree."

Nor are any two people exactly alike. We talk about some people as being like two peas in a pod. If you study peas closely, again you find there aren't two the same in any pod in the world! Isn't God great? The fact that there is anything at all, the design you can see, the intricate mechanism! Even if you look no further than your own body you are led to say, "I praise you for I am fearfully and wonderfully made."

I spent a weekend with a group of doctors – surgeons, and about five professors – and it was frightening! There they were, all producing more and more volumes of literature about the bodies that we are using, and still they don't understand all the secrets of the human body.

I am not sure that one is nearer God's heart in a garden because in a garden you always get the sameness that man has created. Have you noticed that? A flower bed may be very neat and orderly—that is what man does. I know a gardener said, "You should have seen this place when the Lord had it on his own," but even so there is a wonderful variety and a beauty in nature. "Lord, give us eyes to see there is a book who runs may read." But there are some people who can't read — some who can walk through all this and never see the Lord. Why not? Sometimes there are outward limitations. Sometimes there are things in nature that puzzle us and hide God from us.

A lady who had been to see a nature film said, "It's destroyed my faith in God." It studied apparently the natural life of the prairie and showed how species prey on species, and each preys on another, depicting the cruelty and the difficult things to understand. She said, "I can't believe in God if that's what he has made." Some people find difficulty even in nature itself. After a typhoon, tsunami or an earthquake we see much suffering. (See my book *Why Does God Allow Natural Disasters?* for a detailed discussion of this, and a biblical answer).

But I think the main reason why people find the world around us difficult to "read" is an internal factor. It is in their minds, not elsewhere. "Two men looked through prison bars — one saw mud, the other stars." It depends what you are looking for. If you want to read a wonderful poem, read Masefield's *Everlasting Mercy*, the story of Saul Cain and his conversion. When he came to know God, he walked out and every bush was aflame with God. He saw God's handiwork in every leaf.

Someone who helped me a lot when I was just beginning the Christian life had spent his nights in the public house. Until he was converted he never went for a walk in the nearby woods, though afterwards every leaf spoke to him of the Lord. Something had happened inside him and now he could "read the book outside". The Bible would put it like this: "It's only a fool who says there is no God," and: a man who can't see God in what God has made is without any excuse. (See Romans chapter 1.)

Paul wrote: "For since the beginning of the world the invisible attributes of God, his eternal power and divinity, have been plainly discernible through the things that he has made and which are commonly seen and known, thus leaving men without a rag of excuse" (J B Phillips' translation). If a man can say, "I do not believe that anyone made all this," he is a fool and God will call him to account. He has no excuse for that. He may never have been to church and never heard a preacher, but he should know that there is an Almighty Creator who has made everything that is.

But I believe in God as Creator not only because I see it in the "book" outside, not just because there is a "book" I can read as I am driving my car, and as I look at the hills and catch a glimpse of the mighty sea — there is another book that tells me that God is Creator, namely the Bible. From beginning to end it tells me this. I think most people know its first five words: "In the beginning God created...." You find that theme goes right through to the last two chapters of the book. If you can't see it in the world outside then let me show it to you from scripture.

The book of Job depicts a man who grumbled about his lot in life, who complained against God, and forgot that he was addressing the Lord. People do forget this and they say:

"Why does God allow this?" and "Why did God do that?"

The Lord answered Job out of the whirlwind: "Gird up your loins like a man. I will question you and you shall declare to me. Where were you when I laid the foundation of the earth? Tell me if you have understanding. Who determined its measurements? Surely you know. Or who stretched the line upon it? On what were its bases sunk? Or who laid its cornerstone when the morning stars sang together and all the sons of God shouted for joy? Or who shut in the sea with doors when it burst forth from the womb, when I made clouds its garments, and thick darkness its swaddling bands? Have you commanded the morning since your days began, and caused the dawn to know its place?"

So it continues for five chapters, at the end of which Job says, "Behold I am of small account. What shall I answer thee? I lay my hand on my mouth." It is the beginning of worship when you realise that there is a Creator who made all that is. We grumble, we complain, and in our pettiness we are impudent to the Almighty God. God says, "Where were you when I made the world? Can you cause the sun to rise tomorrow morning? I will, but can you?" Remember to whom you are speaking! When you come to worship God, remember who you are meeting — the Creator, the one who made you. Be reverent before him.

The Bible tells us many things about the Creator. It says first that *God made everything that is*. There is not a thing that exists that he didn't make. It tells us, second, that *he made all that out of nothing at all*. It is interesting that there is a special word used for "create" which means to make something out of absolutely nothing. Somebody has asked me, "Will scientists ever be able to create life?" I said no, and I can say that with absolute certainty. They will not have created it, they will have manufactured it out of something else. But the day a scientist can stand and say, "Let there be

15

life," and life appears, then I shall believe science can create.
Science can never create a thing.

The Bible tells us, too, that God made everything that is
in this world *for mankind*. When man conquers the things
that God has made, and uses them for his purposes, that is
his intention. It is not against God's will, it is in his will.
He made it, that we might have dominion over it. All our
science should acknowledge that it is just doing God's will
in conquering the things that he has made for our benefit.

The Bible tells us that when God made everything he made
it *very good*. Here is a little secret: the Bible reveals some
things have gone wrong in nature. The lion was not meant
to eat the lamb. There were not meant to be earthquakes. We
must not blame God for it. When nature left God's hands
it was all right. My car may be all right when it leaves the
factory, but if I treat it badly, forget to service it and handle
it wrongly, I cannot blame another for what has gone wrong.
So here is a most wonderful secret. If I asked you where you
would find the creation in the Bible, I am sure you would
say, "Genesis chapter 1". I would say, "Go right to the
other end." Because here is the wonderful thing that I would
not know through science, philosophy or any other human
channel: one day God is going to take this old universe and
he is going to remake it. At the end of the Bible it says,
"I saw a new heaven and a new earth, for the old one had
passed away." God is not going to patch up this old one, he
is going to make a new one. It is a wonderful thought—that
everything you can see that is made is only temporary. It will
be dissolved; it will be finished with, says the Bible. One
day, the God who made everything you can see is going to
make another great universe.

The only difference, and this is very significant and
brings me to my third point, between his first creation and
the second creation at the end of history — in the first, *man*

16

was the last thing to be made; in the second, man is the first thing to be *re-made*. The wonderful truth is that God is taking lives of ordinary men and women and making them new, ready to inhabit his new universe when he builds it. How do I know that God is Creator? By reading nature, by looking into his book, but above all by looking into myself and asking, "Is he Creator there?"

Let me tell you what I mean. First of all you could find this out with your body. If one of our pieces of household equipment goes wrong we do one of three things with it. If my wife can manage to do so, she asks me to get out my tools and get down to it myself, and I have a "do it yourself" job. Sometimes it works, sometimes it doesn't. If that doesn't work then I might take it to a local repair shop, but it might be beyond them too. Sometimes it has to go right back to the maker.

There are those who know that God is the Creator because their body tells them. Sometimes they are out of sorts and they can put it right themselves: maybe get to bed an hour earlier —that is a "do it yourself" job. Sometimes they are able to get "local repairs" —the doctor puts them on a medicine. But sometimes they need to take that body of theirs right back to the Maker and say, "Lord, you'll have to do something," and he does it. Such a person knows that God, the Creator, still has their body in the hollow of his hand.

But I am concerned far more with the creative power of God in my spirit, not my body. There was once a man who lived in a large house and he found that his bedroom window overlooked a neighbour's bathroom. One night he watched a woman have a bath and he was convicted of this. When he got on his knees afterwards, he said: "Create in me a clean heart O God, and renew a right spirit within me." That is in Psalm 51, the man was King David, and the girl was Bathsheba. But he said, "Create in me," he didn't

17

say, "Clean up this old heart," he didn't say, "Patch up this old life," he didn't say, "Help me to improve," he didn't say, "Help me to conquer this temptation," he was saying: "Lord, I want an act of creation. I've got a dirty heart. Can you create in me a new heart, a clean heart, a right spirit?"

Praise the Lord, he can and he does. There are people who could say, "I know God is Creator because he has created a new life in me, a life that I never thought was possible. He has created a heart that desires him."

Paul says that if anyone is in Christ he is a new creation. I might believe in the Creator because of the fields and the trees around me. I might believe in the Creator because the Bible tells me so and I was told that in Sunday school as a child, but now I know he is the Creator because he has made me a new creation.

That is what becoming a Christian is — not patching up the old but getting a new life; not trying to improve the old life and getting rid of the habits, but taking a new life from the hands of God. This is so new that you can talk in terms of being *born* again. This is what the Bible really is saying: that the Creator of all has made his power available to anyone who will tap it. In Isaiah 40 we have: "Have you not known? Have you not heard? The Lord is the everlasting God, the Creator of the ends of the earth"—but suddenly it comes right down to personal issues and says that he gives strength to the weary, and that those who hope in the Lord will renew their strength.

It is a wonderful thought, that every one of us could be in personal contact with the Creator's resources and know that the power that set the stars in their courses and packed the atom is available to me now. That is how Jesus talked. He said, "Look at nature. Look how God looks after the flowers of the field, look how he feeds the birds of the air. Don't you think he wants to look after you too?"

Walk with the Creator, remember your Creator in the days of your youth, and then walk every day, realising that the Almighty Maker of heaven and earth wants to help you through the day.

Even youths shall faint and grow weary, even young people need God. He steps right in and you *know* he is the Creator because you find you have got the touch of those hidden springs of power in the universe — *for yourself.*

You will notice that I have been feeling my way into talking about Jesus Christ. If anyone is *in Christ* there is a *new creation.*

All that you can find out about the Creator is not enough to make you love him. Can you love the great "architect" of the universe? I don't think so. Can you love the "first cause" of all that is? —to quote a great philosopher. You cannot love a God you *only* find through nature. The Creator may seem somehow impersonal and distant, but I will tell you the better name for God: *Father.* If the great Creator can be my Father then I have all I need.

2

DIVINE, ETERNAL;
FATHERLY GOODNESS

You may discover the peace of God as you walk through the fields and the woods. You may feel you have discovered the majesty of God as you look at the mountains. You may feel that you are in touch with the greatness of God when you look out over the ocean. You may feel that you have seen the glory of God in a sunset, but Jesus said, "Nobody comes to the Father but by me." Those who really know God as Father are those who have come to know Jesus Christ as Saviour.

In Isaiah 57:15, God is described as the High and lofty one who inhabits eternity. In Matthew 7:11 he is described as the Father in heaven who gives good things to those who ask him. If I were to ask a congregation which of these two texts they would prefer me to preach on, I think at least three-quarters would say the second. The first seems a little beyond our understanding, '"The high and lofty one who inhabits eternity" – what on earth does that mean?' some might say. But when we talk about a Father who gives good things to those who ask him, I can begin to grasp that.

I am going to deal with both texts, to try to show you that if we are to come to God in a real way – and know him as he is – we have somehow got to fit in not only the texts that we understand and that are so clear and so simple, but somehow to include in our thinking the things about God that are difficult for us to understand.

We are going into the next four letters and jumbling them just a little — thinking about his *eternal deity* on the one hand and his *fatherly goodness* on the other. One seems like the thing that we just can't grasp or understand but which we need to believe, and the other seems so simple and so lovely that I hardly need to say anything about it.

I begin with the more difficult. One of the most human prophets in the Old Testament was Hosea, whose wife was unfaithful to him, and some of whose children were not his own as the result. You feel that here is a man who understands people. Yet Hosea (11:9) says, "Thus says the Lord, 'I am God and not man.'" One of the things I do find with people who are trying to seek God, and trying to believe in him, is that they are constantly wanting to cut God down to human size. They say: I can't believe in a God I can't understand. Until you can explain this, that, and the other, don't expect me to believe in him. But you cannot cut God down to human size. "I'm God," he says, "not man."

Let me try in simple language to tell you at least three things about God the Bible tells us, which you cannot understand (and which I cannot understand) but which we need to believe. First: God has no body. He is invisible. He is real – we know that. He has a heart, a mind, and a will. But to think that he should have no body! Now I know that the Bible talks about his "arms" — "Underneath are the everlasting arms." I know that the Bible talks about the "ears" of the Lord — "The ear of the Lord is open to the righteous." I know that the Bible talks about the "hand" of the Lord being upon me, but nobody takes that literally.

But we know that these are metaphors – picture language. The Bible does not say God is like you with a body, but: "God is Spirit." Isn't it difficult to think of a person without a body? It is so difficult to feel that someone you cannot see is real, and that is why the Bible states quite clearly:

"Nobody has ever seen God at any time." You don't get on to him through your senses. You can't see him; you can't hear him with your ears; you can't smell him or touch him. None of your five senses can get on to God. That is why you can never *prove* to someone who is sceptical that there is such a being.

Here is another thing the Bible tells us about God that is so difficult to understand: God has no birthdays. We know that we are limited by time— I have a birthday, and so do you. Are you at the age where now you would rather think that you haven't? It will still come around once a year. You began to live on a certain day and there will be a day when you cease to be. We find it very difficult to think in terms of someone who never has a birthday because they had no beginning and no ending.

I promised to give you the answer to a child's question, "Who made God?" I am going to give you the simple, straightforward, truthful answer, but it will depend on your mind whether you accept it or not. The answer is: *God always was, and therefore he never needed to be made*. It is as simple as that. In a sense, it is a self-contradicting question to ask, "Who made God?" because the word "God" means someone who does not need to be made. You are really asking: who made someone who doesn't need to be made? God is from everlasting to everlasting. He inhabits eternity; he never had a beginning, and he will never have an ending. Words that are used of God in scripture are used in our worship: "Forever and ever" —a phrase that recurs in the prophet Isaiah. And: "Throughout all ages, world without end." Only God is without end.

That is the second thing that is so difficult to understand. I have a body but *God has no body, he is Spirit*. If you want to get in touch with him you can't do so through your ordinary senses — you worship in Spirit and in truth. You can never prove to a person who is not in the Spirit that there is such a being.

Thirdly, *God has no bounds*. Remember I am trying to use simple language. The theologians would say, "God is invisible, God is immortal and God is infinite," but these words mean so little. God has no body, God has no birthdays, and God has no bounds. What bounds are set to our life? What bounds are set to my knowledge, for example? Oh I may try, and read, and stuff everything I can into my brain, but there are bounds to what I can know. There are some things I can never know. My knowledge of the past is limited by my memory. The older you get, the more difficult it is to put something else in that you can remember, until you get to the point where you find it easier to remember something that happened forty years ago than something that happened forty days ago. My memory of the present is limited by my information about it. My knowledge of the future is strictly limited. Now can you imagine one who has no boundary to his knowledge of the past, the present or the future?

I was at a football match some time ago and, looking around a crowd of seventy thousand, I thought: I find it almost impossible to believe that God knows every one of these people individually and knows everything about them, even the number of hairs on their head. That was only seventy thousand, and when I think of the billions of people, how can God do this? My little mind can't take it in. Like the psalmist I simply say, "Such knowledge is too wonderful for me. It is high; I cannot attain to it." My mind could never do that, even with one person, but God can do it with millions. It is marvellous. There are no limits to his knowledge.

There is no limit to his *presence*. God is everywhere. He says, "I fill heaven and earth."

"God is not far from each one of us," said Paul when he stood on the hill at Athens. He's not far from any one of us.

Indeed we live and move and have our being in him. Even if you don't know it, you are as close to him as that, for God is everywhere. Heaven is his throne and the earth is his footstool. The universe is small to God. He sits in heaven and his feet are on earth. It means that I could emigrate to Australia, and when I stepped off the boat I could say, "Lord, I'm still with you." He would be just as near to me there as here. What a great God we have!

A little girl prayed one night and said: "Well goodbye, Lord, we're off to Blackpool for our holidays tomorrow." She had a cut down picture of God. She had brought God down to man's size and she couldn't think of a God who could be anywhere or everywhere. She had not yet learned that God has no limit to his knowledge, no limit to his presence.

There is no limit to his power. One day God said to a woman who was one hundred years old, "You're going to have a baby," and she laughed. What did God say to that woman? He said, "Is anything too hard for the Lord? Why did you laugh?" Was it because her idea of God was too limited? This refrain goes right through the scriptures. "Is anything too hard for me?" says the Lord. It is wonderful when you break through, out of the limitations of your little mind and suddenly realise that nothing is too hard for God. The day you come to that faith you have no more problem with miracles. You have no questions when you read what God has done.

The theologians would speak about the omniscience, omnipotence and omnipresence of God. You can take those terms and chew them over, but simply they are saying: there are no limits to God, no limits to his knowledge, no limits of space. I wish I could be in two places at once sometimes, don't you? But if I am in one place I can't be anywhere else, but God is not limited. No wonder in the Old Testament the name of God is "I am who I am". If you gave any other name to God you would be saying that he is like someone else. But God says, "To whom will you liken me? With whom will you compare me?" How can you say, "God is *like* so-and-so"? You just can't do it. God cannot be put in a little neat pigeonhole like that. He says, "My ways are not your ways, neither are your thoughts my thoughts. For as the heavens are high above the earth so are my ways higher than your ways, and my thoughts than your thoughts." So let us get rid of this idea that we have got to bring God down to our size before we can believe. We can explain a lot, or we can try to, but we shall never reduce God down to our size!

Now the problem arises: *how are we ever going to get to know God who is so different from us and so difficult to understand?* Have you noticed that personal relationships are difficult with people you don't understand? Your friends are people you feel you understand. The people you like to be with are those whose wavelength you are on. But how can we get to know God? You might fall down before him in fear and trembling, but could you love one so different?

There are two ways of getting around this difficulty. One is to try to make an image of God that brings him down to your level. There are two sorts of images people have made. One is to make a material image, some grotesque little object of wood, stone or metal and say, "That's god. Now I can understand him. Now I can see him. Now I can touch him. Now I can come and speak to him." The prophets in the Bible laugh at those who try that way of understanding God. They say: If you cut God down to the size of a material image, then you will have to carry him about. He won't carry you. That is a lovely way of pulling people up and making them think. The God that I worship has said: "Even to your grey hairs, I will carry you."

If you try to cut God down to size, into some visible object, some image you can kiss and pray to, that "god" you have made — which isn't actually God — won't be able to help you. It is only a bit of wood or other material, dead, not alive. You may not be guilty of this, but I have noticed that whenever people make an idol or an image it is always of something earthly. It might be grotesque. It might have a dozen arms, yet every arm is a human arm. It might have eyes all over its head, I've seen one like that, yet every eye was an earthly eye. Though these idols were trying to say "this is what God is like", every one of them finished up by being a grotesque conglomeration of human and animal features. You can't get God down to earth that way.

Secondly, there are those who try to make a mental image of God, and who say, "Well I'm not going to accept the God who is portrayed here, I am going to cut him down to size — not in wood or stone, but in ideas." People get a little mental image of God — so small. If you do that you fail to get through to him. Why? Because when you pray you are just praying to your own mental image. Your prayers are to yourself and you will get the answers that *you* give. Mental images don't get God down to our level. Shall I tell you what we need? If we are going to understand the *eternal deity* of God, if we are going to get through to the one who is so different from us, what is needed is *a moral image that we could see*. I mean by that a human life that would so perfectly embody the character of God that you could say to someone, "If you want to know what God is like, look at him," and that is exactly what God provided for us.

He knew that our minds are too small to get up to that. He knew that while we may accept it we cannot understand it. So, in his gracious mercy, God gave us in Jesus Christ "the image of the invisible God." I'm quoting the Bible there. So if you find words like infinite, invisible, immortal, omniscient and omnipresent bewildering, then I say: look with me at *Jesus*; in Jesus you have got the image of the

Christian God. It was the apostle Philip who wanted Jesus to show the disciples God the Father. Jesus said, "Philip, have I been such a long time with you, have you not seen yet? If you have seen me, you have seen him." Now somehow all these things come to the point at which my mind can begin to understand. When I look at Jesus and say, "That is what God is like" I find that this phrase come to my mind. I can see that God is not only one who has *eternal deity* but I can see his *fatherly goodness* now — and that begins to click; that begins to reach my heart.

So I turn now to the fatherly goodness of God. Now I can begin to grasp, but I will never make the mistake of thinking that I have got it all. We must not make the mistake of thinking that when we have grasped one idea of God, we have understood all about him. No, we say we have just begun to understand.

Consider now the fatherly goodness of God as it is revealed in Jesus Christ. I don't think anybody would quarrel with the word "goodness". It is said in Acts 10 of Jesus that he went about doing good. Here was a good man, a good life. But do you realise just *how* good?

One day a young man came to Jesus and he bent down and said, "Good master" — and Jesus said, "Why did you use that word 'good' of me? You know that you ought not use that word except about God. Why did you call me good? None is good but God alone." Jesus' words convey the truth that the goodness in him is the goodness of God. People were seeing in him the image of the invisible God.

Indeed the goodness of Jesus, which people saw, was that of one who was not only man but who was and is God. The people did not realise this. They saw him heal people's bodies, they saw him bring sanity to minds, they saw him bring forgiveness, they saw him raise the dead, they saw him do so many things, and they kept asking: what manner of man is this? We don't understand—he doesn't fit into our categories. There is something more than human here. Bit by bit they came nearer and nearer the truth as they lived with him. Then one day someone said right to his face, "My Lord and my God." The goodness of Jesus was the goodness of God, and for the first time there was a life on earth at which anyone could look and say: that is what God who inhabits eternity is like.

Now let us think about the *fatherly* side. In the Old Testament the favourite name for God is Yahweh, "I am what I am". But Jesus did not tell us to be witnesses to Yahweh (sometimes rendered "Jehovah"). Jesus gave us a different name for God: "Father", and somehow that is a name people are going to understand. You go to someone who never goes to church and ask, "What does the word 'Jehovah' mean to you?" and they will think of a person in a raincoat who knocks at their door. But if you say, "What does the name 'Father' mean to you?" —it means something. It will depend on what their own human father was like. To those who have had at least something of an upbringing in a normal home, you can say, "What does the word 'father' mean to you?" and it means something. Then you can build on that, because Jesus did. He said: if earthly fathers look after their children like this, how much more will your heavenly Father?

He started with something most people can understand. A father looks after his children. If a child is hungry and asks the father for food, will he give him a scorpion? No, fathers don't behave like that. Multiply that by infinity until you get to your heavenly Father and then you see how he gives good things to those who ask. But Jesus never taught the fatherhood of God in a universal sense. He never taught this modern myth of the fatherhood of God and the brotherhood of men, and that we are *all* in God's family. He was most careful to avoid it.

Indeed, I notice this: our Lord never once used the word "Father" in public. If you don't believe me, check up for yourself. Go and read the four Gospels. Never once when the crowds were around did he use the word "Father". It was something almost too sacred to use before the general public.

Three things can help you to understand what the word "Father" means when speaking about God. First: God is the Father of one — and only one — begotten Son. Jesus was the only one who could call him "Father" in the deepest sense. When you look at the life of Jesus, from his very first words as a boy of twelve to his dying words as a man on the cross, you find one word that goes as a scarlet thread all the way through. The boy of twelve speaking to Joseph said, "Didn't you realise that I had Father's business to see to?" His first recorded words. Later, when he comes to his baptism, Jesus does not speak but his Father does, and says, "You are my beloved Son and I am very pleased." All the way though his life whenever he was in a crisis, Jesus went out alone to be with his Father.

When Jesus came to die, he used the goodnight prayer that he had been taught — as a good Jewish boy would before he went to sleep — saying, "Into your hands I commit my spirit." The addition at his death on the cross was one word at the beginning: "Father". If you want to know what God is like as a Father, then look at his only Son. See what Jesus thought of his Father. He made it clear that he had come to tell his hearers what his Father had told him. He had come to do his Father's will. When he wanted to comfort those who were about to be bereaved, he said, "In my Father's house there are many resting places."

The word Jesus used is an interesting one: "Abba", the Jewish word for "Daddy". All the way through his life, "Didn't you know that I must be about my dad's business?" "Dad, into your hands I commit my spirit." I think you realise now why Jesus didn't say much about this in public. It was too sacred, too wonderful and too intimate.

So God has only one *begotten* Son, and we can't just say everybody is a brother because we all have one Father. No, you might go as far to say we are all God's offspring, but not all are sons. Adoption is needed for that.

So we come to the second thing: God has many *adopted* sons. I am one not because I am good enough to be one, but because by the grace of God he adopted me. It is most wonderful to know that God will take a person and adopt them into his family, and say, "Now you're a son." If you go to some stately homes in England you come to a barrier, and see a notice saying: "For members of the family only". You — a member of the general public — cannot go any further beyond that rope. But then you watch, and somebody walks straight through, and you know that they have the privilege.

There is room in God's house for everyone if they will come. There is room for all his adopted sons and daughters. He gives you the privilege for members of the family now. When Jesus, the only begotten Son, is your Saviour and Lord, you have become a son and you have the right to use the same title of God as he did: Abba, Father.

One day Jesus was found praying, and when he had finished, one of his disciples said, "Lord, will you teach us to pray?" Notice that he did not say, "Lord, teach us *how* to pray." It is one thing to be told how to pray, and it is another thing to be taught to pray. Jesus said, "When you pray, say, 'Father....'" He gave this privilege to those who believed in him and accepted him. I must admit I still cringe every time we say the Lord's Prayer in too public a way. "Our Father" is a very deep title to take upon our lips. The God who inhabits eternity, the high and lofty one, infinite, immortal, and yet that is the privilege of the adopted sons.

Thirdly: God has no grandsons. Parents may have been

children of God and called him "Father", but that does not mean you will. Your grandparents may have known the Father in heaven, but that does not mean you will. It is one thing that cannot be passed on by heredity. God only has adopted sons, those who come as individuals to the Lord Jesus Christ and say, "Christ, will you be my Saviour?" They then become a son, an heir; a joint heir with Christ.

I have tried to show you that there are some things in God we cannot understand, yet there are some things in God we can understand. We have wonderfully been given an image of the invisible God in Jesus Christ. When we look at Jesus we see the fatherly goodness of God.

It is absolutely vital that you should hold the two sides together. First, it is vital to your welfare and second it is vital to your worship. Take the first: it is vital to your welfare. Now I can remember the days when I thought my earthly father was omnipotent. Whatever I did, I took it to him and expected him to be able to do something with it. My son went through that stage too. The most impossible situation — and along he came. He broke a toy in pieces irretrievably and he came, "Daddy, can you do something with it?" He would discover, as I discovered, that there are limits to an earthly father's power. He would also discover, as I discovered, that you don't live with your earthly father for ever, that you have got to leave him, and that he is limited to one place and you cannot always turn to him. He will also discover that, in normal circumstances, his father will probably leave this world before he will, and there will be an end to his father.

But if I have a heavenly Father, someone who has no ending, someone who will never disappoint me, someone who is everywhere I go, then you can see what a wonderful Father I have. Do you see what it means for your welfare? There was a little girl sitting in a train and somebody sitting opposite noticed she was by herself, and she said to the little girl, "Aren't you afraid to travel all alone?" She said, "No." The lady said, "Why not?" She said, "Because my daddy's driving this train."

Now if you can face life like this and somebody says, "Why aren't you afraid," and you say, "Because my heavenly Father's got this universe in his hand; my Father is running all this," do you see what a difference this makes? That is why I say that we have to hold together in our thinking not only the things about God we can understand, but also those things we cannot understand but in which we rejoice. Listen to this text which has helped a lot of people through difficulties — it helped my own father through a very serious operation. A fellow patient slipped the paper into his hand just before he went to the operating theatre. On it was written this: "The eternal God is your refuge and underneath are the everlasting arms."

Now I do not understand *eternal* and *everlasting*, but I thank God that the arms of my heavenly Father are everlasting and that my refuge is eternal. Have you got it? It is one thing to believe in a father, and it is another thing to believe in an *everlasting* Father. It's one thing to believe in someone who looks after you; it is another thing to believe in someone who is everywhere looking after you. So the things that we can understand, and the things we can't understand, come together and just fill out our faith with a wonderful *trust*.

We need to keep these two things together in our worship. I have been to some churches where the understanding of God was of him being so far away that the service was cold. It just didn't reach me. I have been to other churches where people were just too pally with God. There was no reverence. They believed in what they could understand, and that was as far as they could see. There was no sense that they were coming to an eternal Father.

3

HOLINESS, INDIGNATION, JUSTICE AND KINDNESS

Here is a passage from Isaiah chapter six. We are not going to stop at v. 8, which is where every public reading of this that I have ever heard has stopped:

In the year that King Uzziah died I saw the Lord sitting upon a throne, high and lifted up; and his train filled the temple. Above him stood the seraphim, and each one had six wings: with two he covered his face, and with two he covered his feet and with two he flew. And one called to another and said, "Holy, holy, holy is the Lord of Hosts; the whole earth is full of his glory!" And the foundations of the thresholds shook at the voice of him who called, and the house was filled with smoke.

And I said, "Woe is me for I am lost; I am a man of unclean lips and I dwell in the midst of a people of unclean lips; for my eyes have seen the King, the Lord of hosts."

Then flew one of the seraphim to me, having in his hand a burning coal, which he had taken with tongs from the altar. And he touched my mouth and said, "Behold, this has touched your lips; your guilt is taken away and your sin is forgiven."

And I heard the voice of the Lord saying, "Whom shall I send, and who will go for us?"

Then I said, "Here am I! Send me."

And he said, "Go, and say to this people: 'Hear and

hear, but do not understand; see and see but do not perceive.' Make the heart of this people fat, and their ears heavy, and shut their eyes; lest they see with their eyes, and hear with their ears, and understand with their hearts, and turn and be healed."

Then I said, "How long, O Lord?"

And he said: "Until cities lie waste without inhabitant, and houses without men, and the land is utterly desolate, and the Lord removes men far away, and the forsaken places are many in the midst of the land. And though a tenth remain in it, it will be burned again, like a terebinth or an oak, whose stump remains standing when it is felled. The holy seed is its stump.

It is one thing to say to God: "Here am I, send me." It is quite another thing to be prepared to deliver the message that God sends you to give. Maybe you have never thought quite like this about God; maybe the whole fullness of the godhead never quite struck you. I hope that by the time we finish the alphabet, you will realise that God is so great.

We began very simply with A-B-C, and I said that God was our **A**lmighty and **B**ountiful **C**reator, but the Bible doesn't use those adjectives about him. It says that he is our *holy* Creator. Then I went on to his **D**eity and his **E**ternity, which make him unlike us. One verse of scripture begins: "I am God and not man," but it continues: "I am God and not man, the Holy One of Israel." We have seen that God is our Father and we rejoice in that, but when Jesus prayed to his own Father he said, "Holy Father." When we pray the Lord's Prayer we must always remember to include, "Holy be your name," or as it is put in our familiar English version: "Hallowed be your name."

We must never forget that the word "holy" needs to be put in front of everything else you say about God. Even to say "God is love" is dangerous unless you add the adjective "holy" because there are so many unholy kinds of love around that we shall not get the right picture. So I am taking the letter "H" but I am also taking two more which are related to it, and I want to teach now about *God's holiness, his indignation, and his judgment.* This will be a fit preparation for *his kindness, love, and mercy.*

God's holiness, his indignation and his judgment—this is a very serious subject. I would not choose it if the Bible had not commanded me to speak about such things; not very "nice" or pleasant, and probably your temperament reacts as well, but it is true. Let us take the word "holy" first. It is a word that is dropping right out of the English language. There are so very few things still regarded as holy.

The expression "holy" is used in different senses. First of all, it is used by some as a swear word. Swearing takes something holy and treats it as profane and to be trampled upon. Therefore, most swear words go straight back to either religion or sex, the two holiest relationships that we know — our relationship with God and our relationship between men and women. There are others who use the word "holy" not in swearing but sarcastically. "He's a holy Joe", "Holier-than-thou attitudes", and they use it as an insult. Indeed, if some people called me a "Holy Joe" I would feel insulted. I would feel that I had given the wrong impression or that they were saying something nasty about me. Isn't this a tragedy — that this word, which belongs to God and describes God should be used either in swearing or a sarcastic manner? More overseas than in England, the word "holy" is often used in a superstitious sense, meaning people, places or objects are to be avoided because they are mysterious, because they are uncanny and seem to be associated with supernatural power. That is beginning to get a little nearer.

Then there are those who use the word "holy" simply to

describe something sacred. Jacob at Bethel said, "This is a holy place." Moses, when he saw the bush, was told, "Take your shoes off, this is a holy place," meaning it is a sacred place. A book was written by a German philosopher called Rudolf Otto, which has influenced very profoundly many theologians in this country. He called the book The Idea of the Holy, and he coined a word —"numinous". What he meant was a place, object or person who gives you a sense of "don't touch; keep away". That is a sacred use, but it is still not the scriptural use.

The scriptural use of the word "holy" means far more than supernatural power. It means supernatural purity. It is the very character of God, and when you say "God is holy" you mean God is cleaner than you can imagine. God is utterly pure, and this is something that we have never known, so it is so difficult for us to imagine it.

I am going to try to make this real for you. May I begin by asking two very simple questions? First, what would it be like to meet a really holy person? Would you like them or dislike them? Would you feel drawn towards them or repelled by them? When Jesus was on earth, for the first time in human history a really holy person was living among people. We can answer the question by asking, "How did men and women feel about a holy person called Jesus?"

The answer is very simple. At first they were attracted; they came in their thousands. They loved him; they were drawn to him; they wanted to be with him — but very soon this gave way to a discomfort. They began to feel when they got nearer to him a little uncomfortable. They began to feel a little dirty; they began to feel a little sinful. They began to say this kind of thing, and one disciple said, "Depart from me for I am a sinful man." In simple English: "I'm not for the likes of you." The upshot of it was that within three years people hated him. Now that is how many folk react to a really holy person. At first they might feel drawn. Then they feel uncomfortable, and they finish up hating him. That happened to Jesus. His holiness had this effect. That is why Jesus said, "They hated me and they will hate you." But the hate will be in proportion to your holiness.

"Whoever would live a godly life in Christ Jesus shall suffer persecution," said Paul, and the hatefulness from others meets holiness if it is real.

When Isaiah was all alone in the temple one day, he was thinking about God, and suddenly he said, "God is holy, holy" and he realised that he was a man of unclean lips. He had not realised that you can be a dirty person in what you *say* as well as in what you *do*. Suddenly he realised. Woe is me; I am lost.... That was not the end of the story. God's holiness reached down and cauterized it, and burnt it out of his lips. Isaiah could be made holy by God.

The other question that might get us into the sense of the word "holy" is this: what would a really holy person feel if they met me? Does that ever strike you? What would that person feel if they met me and if they knew everything about me? Again, it is so difficult to imagine, because I have never been completely holy and so I don't know. We'll have to start with the Bible and ask: "How does God feel about me when he meets me?" I find that in the Psalms and Isaiah, Jeremiah, Ezekiel, Daniel, Micah, Nahum, Habakkuk, Zephaniah, every one of these books, it says that when God meets man he is *indignant*.

That is why I use the letter "I" at this point. When holiness meets something that is not holy, then indignation is the immediate result, and that is a biblical word. Do you remember when Jesus got angry? Do you remember when he whipped some traders out of the temple? That was holy, righteous *indignation*.

Let us go back to the beginning. God made a world. He

fashioned it with his hands and he completed it and then he looked at it and he said, "That's good." He put trees and flowers in it, and animals, birds and fish, and he said, "That's good." Then he put men in it and completed his work and said, "That's very good. Now stay that way." Chapter two of Genesis says that, and: don't let the knowledge of evil spoil this. And you know what happened.

God looks down at a world that left his hands a very good world, and it is not a very good world now. I tremble for the children —realising what kind of a world they really live in. But do you realise what God feels when he looks down? He is indignant; of course he is! He made it beautiful, and mankind has ruined it! He left it very good and look what people have done with their suspicion, hatred, gossip and cruelty.... We are vandals in God's universe, and until we have realised that, every one of us, we shall never begin to be holy, because I have added my share to the world's problems. I haven't reduced them. I have added my share of self-centredness, temper and impatience, and so have you. No wonder God is indignant. He is described by one prophet as, "The God who is of purer eyes than to behold iniquity." He can't bear to look at it. I don't know if you have ever felt as holy as that. It is a rare human experience but God is like that the whole time.

Therefore, I come to the question which Nahum asks. "Who can stand before his indignation?" Who can face an angry God? What is this anger going to result in? The answer is, and I come to my third letter — it must result in Judgment. A holy God who is indignant *must* go on to judgment. We must take this very seriously. Against this backcloth we can come to the glorious news that he is kind, loving, and merciful. You will never understand his sheer kindness unless you have understood that *God is the Judge of all the earth*.

How do we know he is Judge? The answer is very simple—because of what he has done in the past, because of what he is doing now, and because of what he is going to do in the future. I don't like speaking about this. I don't like preaching about it, but it is there and if I am to be true to him and face him one day as a preacher and teacher, I must speak of these things.

Take the past: the historical records of the Old Testament contain some remarkable examples of the moments when God's indignation reached boiling point and boiled over. Consider Sodom and Gomorrah and two neighbouring towns — there is nothing left of them but a graveyard. There is no man or woman living there. Why? The very word "sodomy" —look it up in your English dictionary and you will find out why—because God reached the point where his indignation was such that he said, "I must judge these cities" —four of them, and they have gone altogether.

So has Jericho. It is a ruin and there is nobody living in the old Jericho. There is a town of that name today, but that is a mile and a half away; it is a different place. Jericho has gone. Babylon is gone, and God said, "Nobody will ever live in you again." Do you know that Arab carriers would not stay within the walls of Babylon or Nineveh at night for fear of the "jin", the "evil spirits"? Tyre has gone. These were individual towns that so offended God's holiness that his indignation spilled over in judgment.

There was once a whole society which suffered the same thing, in the days of Noah. Here was a society living purely at the physical level. They never got above it. They ate, they drank, and they lived to satisfy only their physical desires. That is the level at which God's indignation bubbled over. He said, "You're not living for the things that I meant you to live for," and therefore the immediate result was that violence filled the earth. This is as up to date as our news, isn't it? When people live for material things alone and physical things alone, violence will fill the earth. This is today, but Noah's society was completely obliterated except for eight people.

There were also individuals like the man Achan and like the woman Jezebel, so the Bible is full of enough examples to tell you that there comes a point where God's indignation boils over into judgment.

That is the past, what about the present? Can we discern his judgments today? Yes! At a social level. Read Romans chapter 1 and it reads like the present day, when it says, "When men give God up, God gives men up...." The immediate result: perverted minds and perverted bodies; unnatural relationships between men and men, and women and women. I challenge you to study that chapter in Romans. God's judgments are in the earth today, and without being an alarmist or exaggerating, I do believe our nation is under the judgment of God in the light of Romans 1. His indignation reaches a certain point, and when we consider the opportunities that this nation of ours has had, we do not deserve anything less. There is so much theft, cruelty, exploitation, aggression and violence.

Let us turn to the future. Paul, when he stood on Mars hill, said that God has appointed a day when he will judge the world. There is a day coming when all the wicked will be dealt with by God. There is a day coming when every secret will be revealed; when all we have done and all we have said must be faced. This will be the final and most searching day of all.

Somebody might ask: "Is this the God and Father of our Lord Jesus Christ? Is this the God that Jesus believed in?" My answer is, "Yes, it is," and I give you five reasons why I believe this is the God of Jesus. There has been a false dichotomy produced in the twentieth century between the

"God of the Old Testament" and the "God of the New"; as if they are different Gods. Somebody asked me, "Do you believe everything the Bible says about God?" When I said yes, he looked at me strangely. I do, and I believe that everything I have been stating here, Jesus believed. Let me tell you why.

First of all, Jesus had a Bible, and his Bible was the Old Testament—he had no other. That was the Bible in which he was brought up, and that is the Bible to which he set his seal, and it is the Bible from which he quoted.

Reason number two: within the New Testament itself you have the clearest possible picture of a God who is holy and indignant and judging. In the last book in the New Testament, the book of Revelation, which is a book written by Jesus, it claims to be the word of Jesus; the risen ascended Jesus speaking to the church, and that is the God he portrays there.

Reason number three: in the New Testament epistles, Paul talks of the day of wrath when God will judge the secrets of men according to my gospel —and there is no other gospel. This is the good news. It must be bad news before it is good news.

Fourth reason: in Matthew, Mark and Luke, Jesus himself quotes as historical events the judgments on Noah, the judgments on Sodom and Gomorrah, the judgment on Nineveh. Therefore we must take them seriously.

The fifth and final reason is simply that Jesus himself, in his own words, spoke of this kind of God. I want to remind you of some words of Jesus, just three verses: "For as the Father has life in himself, so he has granted the Son also to have life in himself, and has given him authority to execute judgment because he is the Son of Man. Do not marvel at this, for the hour is coming when all who are in the tombs will hear his voice and come forth: those who have done good to the resurrection of life, and those who have done evil to the resurrection of judgment." Those are the words of Jesus. This is the God and Father of our Lord Jesus Christ.

There is a way out, there is a way to meet a holy God. There is a way of forgiveness, there is a way of becoming holy as he is holy. There is a way for man to rise. There is a way — and the God who is holy, the God who is indignant when he meets anything that is not holy, the God who must judge the vandals of his universe who have ruined what he made—that God is kind, and loving and merciful and does not take any pleasure at all in the death of the wicked. He is too holy to do that, and he has provided Jesus Christ.

"It is of thy mercies," says the book of Lamentations, "that we are not consumed; your mercies which are new every morning." It is because of this that we dare to take bread and wine in our meetings, and remember that mercy has triumphed over wrath, and that the judgment which was due to every one of us has been turned away and put upon Jesus Christ. He has faced that indignation and that holiness for us, and made possible the forgiveness that makes us new creatures.

God's holiness, his indignation and his judgment are as clearly seen in the cross as his kindness, his love and his mercy.

4

KINDNESS, LOVE
AND MERCY

Once you were under God's curse and doomed forever
for your sins. You went along with the crowd and were
just like the others—full of sin; obeying Satan, the mighty
prince of the power of the air, who is at work right now
in the hearts of those who are against the Lord. All of us
used to be just as they are; our lives expressing the evil
within us, doing every wicked thing that our passions or
evil thoughts might lead us into. We started out bad—
being born with evil natures and were under God's anger
just like everyone else. But God is so rich in mercy; he
loved us so much that even though we were spiritually
dead and doomed by our sins, he gave us back our lives
again when he raised Christ from the dead. Only by his
undeserved favour have we ever been saved, and God
lifted us up from the grave into glory along with Christ
where we sit with him in the heavenly realms, all because
of what Jesus did. And now God can always point to us as
examples of how very, very rich his kindness is as shown
in all he has done for us through Jesus Christ. Because of
his kindness you have been saved through trusting Christ,
and even trusting is not of yourselves. It too is a gift from
God. Salvation is not a reward for the good we have done,
so none of us can take any credit for it. It is God himself
who has made us what we are and given us new lives

from Christ Jesus. And long ages ago, he planned that we should spend these lives in helping others.

Ephesians 2:1–10

Did you notice that three words occur in this short passage—*Kindness, Love and Mercy*, our next three letters of the alphabet. People are childish with the Bible. They pick a text up and say, "Oh, isn't that lovely? I'll keep that, I'll write it down." Then they pick up another text and they think, "Dear me, I don't like what that says about God. I'll throw it away." The tragedy is they never get the whole picture, and they never see God as he really is in all his fullness—the fullness of the godhead. But I am quite sure that nobody will have any objections to these three words! Now while this is the loveliest part of the picture of God, it is the hardest to preach. Indeed, these are three things that are very difficult to put into words. Our understanding of them usually comes through deeds, actions. Therefore, if I am going to help you to understand the kindness, love and mercy of God, I must describe the deeds of God through which we know these three things.

In other words, these three virtues are to be *practised* rather than preached. Take *kindness*: now we all know what we mean by kindness, but how many of us could define it? I am quite sure you would say of someone else, "They are kind," but if I came back at you and said, "What do you mean?" I think you would have to think some time before you could say. You just *know* instinctively that person is kind.

Kindness includes being considerate. It means someone who cares, and someone who goes on caring and is prepared to care for someone who is unworthy. This kindness is there in the Bible. You find it as much in the Old Testament as the New. One of the most common words in the Old Testament is "loving kindness", and it occurs most frequently in a little book called Hosea, to which you could give the subtitle The Prophet and the Prostitute, because it struck the headlines in Israel when this prophet married this woman. Everybody knew what he was, and what she was, and it really caused a stir. Sure enough, the predictions of the gossips came true and she left him and ran away with another man. But Hosea went looking for her in the streets until he found her. He didn't recognise her when he found her, but he brought her back. Through this personal experience in his own life, the preacher Hosea saw what loving kindness really meant, and he was able to preach about it because he had practised it. His message was that God is like this: Israel is an unfaithful wife to God, but God still shows his loving kindness.

When we turn to the New Testament it is even more clear. You have heard of the Sermon on the Mount, but have you read the Sermon on the Plain? That is in Luke chapter 6, and here is one paragraph from it. Jesus said, "But love your enemies and do good and lend, expecting nothing in return, and your reward will be great and you will be sons of the Most High, for he is kind to the ungrateful and the selfish. Be merciful even as your Father is merciful." Did you notice the three words again?

This is the teaching of Jesus, but I commend to you Paul's letter to Titus, in which the apostle writes of the goodness and the loving kindness of God appearing in our Saviour. You will never understand how kind God is until you look at Jesus.

There are four supreme examples of the kindness of God in Jesus. *First, that he came at all.* That he was prepared to go and live somewhere to save people, and to live somewhere that was not nearly as nice as the place he had lived.

I heard of a Christian in Cardiff who used to go and visit the poorest part of the city. He used to climb the steps in the tenement blocks, call on people and talk to them about the love of God. One day he was standing outside the door of one of the flats after he had gone out, and he heard the woman inside say to a neighbour who was visiting, "It's all very well for him to come and talk about the love of God, but he doesn't live here, he lives in a nice house the right side of town." He sold his house on the right side of town and he went to live in that block. The loving kindness of God our Saviour appeared in the fact that Jesus left his lovely home and came to mankind.

We see the kindness of God in what he did for people— the fact that he did what he did. He went about doing good. Jesus was kind. We see it in the fact that he stayed to the end. He could have stepped back into heaven from the Mount of Transfiguration but he didn't, he came down into the valley again, and having loved his own, he loved them to the end. That was kind. We see it in the death that he died, the greatest kindness that has ever been done to human beings. Here then is the first great truth—the sheer kindness of God. But what lies behind this kindness? What lies behind the kind acts of God in Jesus Christ? The answer is his love.

This is so debased a word. It is used of some things that ought to be thrown in the dustbin as well as some of the highest acts of which we are capable—love. What does it mean? For a deeper look at this, see my short books entitled *Is John 3:16 the Gospel?* and *The God and the Gospel of Righteousness*. In them I explain the various meanings of the words used about the love of God, which stem from different meanings of several Greek words, all rendered in English translations by the one word "love".

When we say "God is love", our meaning must be scriptural not sentimental, not about feelings. It is essentially something of the *will*. It is therefore something that can be commanded. You can't turn on your feelings, but you can say in the scriptural sense "Thou shalt love thy neighbour," and you can say in the scriptural sense, "Thou shalt love the Lord thy God." It is not an emotion because you can't control your emotions. It is something much deeper.

When we ask about what kind of love God has shown, according to the Bible, we find four kinds: his love for his only Son, his love for the Jews, his love for the world, and his love for me. When you understand those things, you understand the astonishing statement that God is love. It helps us to see that God is three persons. Only if you believe in the Trinity can you say "God is love". Only if you believe that even before he created the universe God was already three persons in a loving relationship can you say that he *is* love. It is very moving to see the love of a father and a son, isn't it? But you have never seen real love until you have seen the heavenly Father and the heavenly Son. Jesus was always talking about it. When Jesus was baptised, God the Father affirmed his love for Jesus, his Son. Later, Jesus said, "The Father loves the Son and shows him what he is doing," and later still Jesus said on the night before he died, "As the Father loves me, I love you."

The second love in the Bible is *the love of God for the Jews*. I am a Gentile but I want to put this as tactfully and yet as realistically as I can: not many people love the Jews. In fact, they have probably been the most disliked people on the face of the earth, but God loves them. Why did God love the Jews? Listen to the answer in the Bible: "For you are a people holy to the Lord your God. The Lord your God has chosen you to be a people for his own possession out of all the peoples that are on the face of the earth. It was not because you were more in number than any other people that the Lord set his love upon you and chose you."

Then why was it? "For you were the fewest of all peoples, but it is because the Lord loves you."

That may sound a strange argument to you. Why does

God love the Jews? The answer is not because of anything in the Jews, but *because God loves them*. Why does God love you today? Is it because you are lovely or lovable? We can try to find the reason for God's love, but we can't. Why does God love someone like me? I can't understand that! I stand amazed at the love Jesus offers me. I can only explain it by the fact that he loves. What have the Jews got that others hadn't? Nothing! But God loved them because he loved them.

Which brings me to the third love revealed in the Bible — God's love for the whole world. What is there in this sinful, selfish human race that God finds lovable? Again — nothing! But we can say that God loved the world, because we see what he did for us: *once, in the sacrifice of Jesus on the cross*.

How can he pay any attention to me? The Bible also speaks of God's love for the individual, and it comes right down to the point where you can speak of *the Son of God who loved me and gave himself for me*.

On Remembrance Sunday this text is quoted: "Greater love has no man than this, that a man lay down his life for his friends." I don't want to belittle this or upset anyone, but not everybody who was killed in the war *laid down* their lives. They were all prepared to, but they all tried very hard to save them. There were a few who deliberately laid down their lives. I have heard some stories of those who quite deliberately chose to do this. It wasn't all those who were killed, although they all knew the risk that they ran, but most hoped that they would get back home.

Captain Oates was a man who laid down his life for his friends, walking out of a snow-covered tent in the Antarctic. He laid down his life for his friends because he knew that his physical condition was holding back the others, but that is as far as man can go in his love. Here is the contrast, and let us never quote that text as if to suggest that that love of man is enough to get a man to heaven. It isn't big enough. The love that will get a man to heaven is this: God commends his love towards us in that while we were yet sinners, enemies, rebels, Christ died for us.

A man can lay down his life for a friend, but only God could lay down his life for an enemy. A man could lay down his life for someone he loved, but only God could lay down his life for someone who hated him, and this is the love of God. Just as a volcano erupting reveals the fire that burns in the heart of the earth, the cross reveals the fire of love that burns in the heart of God all the time.

Now we move on to the *mercy* of God. This is the easiest word to define. To put it at a humorous level, a man went to have his portrait painted, and said to the artist, "Will this do me justice?" The artist replied, "It's not justice you need, it's mercy!" The important thing is this: *justice is what I deserve; mercy is what I do not deserve.*

The whole point of the parable of the Good Samaritan is not that the Samaritan did a good deed for someone but that he showed mercy to someone—and that is a very different thing. Why was it a Samaritan? Because Jews and Samaritans didn't speak to each other, and that Jew was walking down the road from Jerusalem to Jericho. Why? To avoid meeting the Samaritans! He was making a journey from southern Israel to northern Israel, and the normal road went right through Samaritan country. He was going sixty more miles out of his way—down to Jericho, up the other side of the Jordan and back into Galilee. If he met a Samaritan he wouldn't speak to him, he would spit. Y*et the Samaritan going down that road saw a man whom he knew would not thank him and he showed mercy.*

In the era of apartheid in South Africa, I read of a white man who was trapped at the bottom of a gold mine. The roof had caved in. Nobody could get in until a black African said,

"I will go in," and he went in, risking his life. They thought he would never get out, but he dragged that white man out. The white man was completely unconscious and far gone, so they rushed him to the hospital and they saved him. When he came round, they said to this white man, "Would you like to meet the man who saved you?" He said, "Yes, I want to thank him," so they called the black African in, and when he came in to the room the white man turned his face to the wall and wouldn't speak.

You may think that is extreme, but we are all capable of this kind of thing. I want to say that if that white man were trapped again in the mine, and that African said, "I'll go in and get him a second time," he would be showing mercy. The first time was a good deed; the second time would have been mercy because it would not have been deserved. That is why Jesus said it was a Samaritan who helped that Jew. Jews have no dealings with the Samaritans, but he helped him; he showed mercy.

We have now reached a state in our thinking, in Britain particularly, where the word "mercy" is dropping right out of our speech, and in its place has come the word "right". *The Bible says that we should talk of mercies. Everything we get is a mercy, not a right. Even my life itself is not a right, it is a mercy. I don't have a right to live considering the commandments of God I have broken.*

"It is of the mercies of God that we are not consumed," says Lamentations, just in front of the phrase, "Great is thy faithfulness. Thy mercies are new every morning."

Your health is a mercy, not a right. These are mercies, not rights, and not just our physical, material blessings, but the spiritual blessings which we enjoy are mercies of God. If you know God's kindness, if you know God's love, that's not because it's a right; it's a mercy.

In the middle of the tabernacle where they worshipped

God in the Old Testament, there was a piece of furniture called the "mercy seat" to remind everyone who came there to worship that they didn't deserve a thing. When we come to the prophets we find this kind of phrase: "Who is a God like unto thee, pardoning iniquity? Thou wilt cast all our sins into the depths of the sea." Down the Thames every day there used to go barges called sludge vessels, and they are taking our waste, our filth, out to sea and dumping it in the depths so that it wouldn't poison us. The mercy of God takes the sludge from our souls and takes it out to the ocean and drops it in the depths of the sea—that is mercy.

"The Lord is merciful and gracious, slow to anger and abounding in steadfast loving kindness," says the Psalm. "He does not deal with us according to our sins, nor requite us according to our iniquities. For as the heavens are high above the earth so great is his love toward those who fear him, and as far as the east is from the west, so far does he remove our transgressions from us."

So in the New Testament God is called the Father of mercies; he is described as being rich in mercy; as being merciful. "Let us therefore with confidence boldly approach the throne of grace...." Why? To find mercy.

The only people that God can really bless in church are those who come and say, "God be merciful to me, a sinner." I have taught in this chapter about the kindness, love, and mercy of God, but this is the right order: mercy, love and kindness. It is only when you start with God's mercy and say "God be merciful to me" that you will discover that he loves you. It is only when you have got through to his love that you will find that he is being kind to you day by day.

I finish with a story, and confess, frankly, it is an emotional and romantic story, but it gets my point across and it has the virtue of being true. A girl in the Midlands lived with her parents and played in the garden, at the bottom of which was the main railway line to London. She often used to climb the apple tree at the bottom of the garden and watch the trains go to London. There came a day when she grew up and became a teenager, and she said to her parents, "I'm sick of you, you just hedge me about with what I can't do and what I mustn't do. I'm fed up with living here. I'm going to be free, I'm going to leave you. I'm going to go to London to live there," so she left.

She went down and down and down. She ruined her life physically, mentally and spiritually—it had been a godly home. Finally she found herself on the Thames embankment one night, determined to finish it all. There was nothing left to live for, and she was only in her twenties. She decided one last thing to try before she did away with herself — to write to her parents and tell them the whole sordid story and say, "I will come on the train to the town and I'll pass the garden. If you will have me back," she said, "Will you hang something white on the apple tree?" Well she went, and as she drew near she didn't know whether to look or not. Then she did, and the whole tree was ablaze with sheets, pillow cases, everything. God loves like that.

5

NAME; ONE GOD

In Exodus chapter 3 the name of God is mentioned for the very first time in the Bible.

Moses said to God, "If I come to the people of Israel and say to them, 'the God of your fathers has sent me to you,' and they ask me, 'What is his name?' what shall I say to them?"

God said to Moses, "I AM WHO I AM." And he said, "Say to the people of Israel, 'I AM has sent me to you.'" God also said to Moses, "Say this to the people of Israel, 'The Lord, the God of your fathers, the God of Abraham, the God of Isaac, and the God of Jacob, has sent me to you.' This is my name forever, and thus I am to be remembered throughout all generations."

What's in a name? Well, a great deal if you buy one of those books in which you can see what your name means. I remember the time my wife and I got such a book on the occasion of our firstborn's arrival, and we did it very scientifically. We each went into a separate room with the book, one after the other, and made a short list of those that appealed to us. Then we came together and saw what was common to the short list, which brought it down to about seventeen. Then we sort of went apart again and reduced that list and came together and it was really quite a process.

Is a name more than a mere label? Of course, it is a useful label to distinguish you from anyone else. If you ever meet a policeman in the course of his duty, which I hope you won't, one of the first things he'll say when he takes out his notebook is, "Your name, please." That's your label. It will enable him to get in touch with you again, even if you don't want him to, but that's what the name means. The name of God means I can get in touch with God again, but is it just a label? Is it just a kind of address?

Well the meaning of a name will depend very much on who gives it and why. The names we all bear are names that were given to us by our parents. The name tells us very much more about our parents than it does about us. In a sense, that is a little unfair. We all get to the point where we want to have our own name. I think most teenagers pass through a stage somewhere between about fourteen and eighteen when they decide to be known by another name, or they would like their second name instead of their first. You have been through this if you are a parent. They are saying, "I want to be me. I don't want to be what you want me to be, I want to be what I want to be," and so they say, "I'll have my name and not the one you gave me."

Of course, many of the names we use are expressions of hope for the person. We call a little child Joy and it's a bit disappointing if she turns out to be morose and moody all her life! But you see, we want our own name because we want the name to express much more what we are. Nicknames come a little nearer to that meaning because these are names given by our contemporaries, not our parents. I am sure you were at school with "Fatty" and all the rest of them!

God's name was not given to him by anyone except himself. He is saying: whenever you hear this name I want you to think of me and no-one else; whenever you hear this name I want you to understand what I am like. So he gave himself a name — and he has told us to *hallow* it, as we recall from the Lord's Prayer. Part of hallowing his name means that we give it to no-one else. If we are going to keep God's name holy, as it ought to be kept holy, we should never apply it to another person. "Hallowed be thy name" — we will keep it just for you, Lord.

The first point to make is this: "God" is not God's name. The word translated "God" in the Old Testament is from the Hebrew word "El", which simply means a supernatural power. We use the word "God" almost as a name for God simply because for centuries in this country we have been taught that there is only one. Even the names of the days of our week should remind us that there was a time when in England if you had said, "Do you believe in God?" the reply would have been, "Do you mean do I believe in the god "sun" who is worshipped on Sunday, or the god "moon" who is worshipped on "Moon day" (or Monday), or the god "woden" who's worshipped on Wodensday, or the god "thor" who is worshipped on Thorsday, or "saturn" who is worshipped on Saturnday?" —and you would have realised that you shouldn't have used the word "god".

In fact, the word "god" is simply a description. It is not the name, and therefore it doesn't really matter whether a person believes in "god" or not; it depends *which* god they believe in. If you went up to a Hindu and said, "Do you believe in God?" he would rightly say, "Which one?" You would then have to name the god you were thinking of in your question. Now this was the situation in Bible times and Moses, brought up in the court of Pharaoh, knew perfectly well that in Egypt they believe in many gods. So when he was sent to Egypt, and God said, "Tell them I'm going to get them out of there," he said, "Well who shall I say called? I don't even know your name and I don't know what to say."

God said, "I will tell you my name."

The basic meaning of the word "god" signifies *power*. Sometimes in the Hebrew language it was extended to a longer word—*El Shaddai*, which means "God Almighty" and that just underlines the power, but that is all it does mean. Simply to believe in God is to believe in a power greater than ourselves behind the universe. It isn't to say very much about God at all. It is not enough.

The extraordinary thing is that in the Bible the word "god" occurs far more often as a plural word than a singular, even when it is applied to our God. In the ratio of eight to one, it says "Gods" instead of "God". We could translate: "In the beginning Gods created the earth, and Gods said, 'let there be light,' and Gods said, 'let there be....'" And, "Gods said, 'Let us make man in our own image.'" Here is a mystery.

So in a sense we have to say to people: "Do you believe in Gods?" —if we were really going to be biblical, because we now know that God is more than one person, he is three persons in one God. If he wasn't, love would not be possible, and love would not be real. We have already seen that before there was any universe, before there were any human beings to love, God was (and is) love because he was more than one person. If I didn't believe in the Trinity, I could not believe in love either, because I would say there's no reality in love. It's just your hormones and your glands. But I can believe in love because God was and is more than one, and yet was and is one.

The second thing is this: we do not know his name today. This may seem surprising when I can also say that his name is used 6,700 times in the Bible, yet you don't know it and neither do I. Now here is a conundrum for you. Let me explain. It was given to Moses at the burning bush, and God said: Moses, I will tell you my name, and when they ask you, you tell them this. He then said something, and none of us really knows what it is. Written down in the Old Testament are four letters: JHWH. That is all we have got. We don't know how to spell it, we don't know how to pronounce it, and we are not completely sure of its meaning. I say we don't know how to spell it and I have just given you the four letters, but you realise that that is an unpronounceable word.

The difficulty with J-H-W-H is that the letters in between are missing, as in normal Hebrew writing. Those who read it at the time knew perfectly well what came in between. Some people have said, "Well all right, let's put in our own letters," and so they have put in an "e," an "o", and an "a", in that order and they have got "Jehovah", but actually we don't know how to spell it.

Furthermore, we don't know how to pronounce it, because "j" is certainly not pronounced in Hebrew as a "j" but as a "y" and the nearest that scholars can get to it is "Yahweh". So is that his name? You see the problem? Now surely the answer to the problem is to make for the nearest Jew and say, "Would you tell us how to pronounce this word?" But the tragedy is that for a whole period of centuries, the Jews never pronounced it, and even they cannot tell you how to say it.

So how can we exalt his name together when we don't even know how to say it? How can we say, "Hallowed be thy name," when we don't even know what it is? In fact, it is a name that we hardly ever use in worship. But there is a wonderful scriptural answer to this problem which I hope will make all things as clear as day, and tell you how to hallow his name, and how to exalt his name together.

Why did the Jews stop saying this name? Well, a fear turned into a phobia. What do I mean by that? Well, my little children had a fear of traffic. I deliberately taught them that fear. I hope they will always have that fear and that they will be very careful crossing the sort of major road such as was outside our front door at one time, with ten thousand cars a day going past! I hope they will always fear the traffic, but if they developed a phobia, they would never cross the road. Do you see the difference? There are many Christians who are so afraid of becoming worldly that they have contracted out of the world and a fear has become a phobia. The Jews, when they read the third commandment, saw this, "Thou shalt not take the name of the Lord thy God in vain." You must never use it in a wrong way. "The Lord will not hold him guiltless who takes his name in vain." They thought the safest way was never to mention it. A healthy fear of using the name wrongly became a phobia. By the time of our Lord, they hardly ever used the name of God. They still knew how to say it, but they hardly dared to use it. If somebody used it, they waited for lightning from heaven to strike them dead. So it died right out — even the Jews can't say it.

Well can we understand what this word of four letters "J-H-W-H" means? Yes, I think we can. It comes from the verb *hayah*, which means *to be*, so there are three alternatives in the RSV Bible: "I Am Who I Am"; "I Am What I Am", "I Will Be What I Will Be". You could choose any of those, but you've got the message — it means "I Am".

What a peculiar name. What does that say to you? I believe God gave this name to himself for two reasons. One was for what it did say, and one was for what it didn't say, and he chose it very carefully. What does it say? It tells me first that God is unique. You can't ever give him a name that will compare him to anything or anyone else. "I Am What I Am," he says — you can't give me a name; you can't describe me; I am me; I'm not like you; I'm unique.

It tells me, secondly, that God is *sufficient* —you can't add anything to me; you can't subtract anything from me; I am self-sufficient.

It also tells me that God is *unchangeable*. I am one thing on Sunday and another thing on Monday morning, as my wife knows —and so are you. I can't say "I Am" of myself because I am not always the same. I have my moods and so have you, but God says: "I Am." This says to me that I will meet the same God on Monday morning as I met on Sunday evening. He is unchangeable and indeed at one point, the prophet Micah says in the name of God: "I, YHWH, change not." I Am What I Am. You may change; I don't. It tells me that God is holy.

It also tells me that God is *eternal*; that he *always is*; that he did not need to be made or to start—"I Am."

So this is what the name says, but I also believe that God chose this name for himself for what it didn't say. It was precisely because he could fill the name with meaning. The interesting thing is that in the Old Testament God is forever adding a phrase to his name. He says, "I'm not just YHWH, I Am What I Am, I Am YHWH Jireh" —which means: "I am your provider." He said that to Abraham when Abraham nearly killed Isaac. He said, "I am YHWH Rapha" —which means, "I am your healer"; "I Am What I Am Healer". He said, "YHWH Nissi" —which means: "I am your banner when you are fighting a battle. You don't need a flag, you just need me: "I Am What I Am Banner." He said, "YHWH Shalom" —which means, "I am your peace"; "I Am What I Am, I'm your peace." He said, "YHWH Ra'ah" —which means one of the loveliest: "I am your Shepherd." He said, "YHWH Tsidkenu" —which means: "I am your righteousness; if you want to be good, you need me." He said, "YHWH Shamma" —which means: "I am your everlasting presence"; "I Am What I Am, and I'll always be with you."

Do you see how he filled the name? Always saying, "I Am What I Am," and then adding something that filled out the meaning and told you what he was. All these double names come through the pages of the Bible to us. So this is his name and that is why when the Jews went to the temple to worship

God they said: "O YHWH, our Lord. How excellent is your name in all the earth" (Psalm 8).

Then why don't we use this name? Why don't we use it much more often than we do? Why do we say "God" so often and say this word so little, at least if we know roughly how to say it and roughly what it means?

Sometimes the Jehovah's Witnesses call. They believe that not only is it a tragedy, but it is the greatest error in the Christian church that we no longer use God's name. This is the main thing they have come to tell you. They quote a text from Isaiah 43:10, "'You are my witnesses,' says Jehovah." Of course, we know perfectly well that whatever else God's name was, it wasn't "Jehovah", but even so, are they right in saying to us that we have made a fundamental error and they are the only true witnesses in the world as the ones who witness to God's *real* name. Either they are right and we are all wrong, or there is some other explanation. I want to say very humbly without suggesting that I am judging them in this, that I believe it is they who have made the mistake. They would say that it is largely a matter of translation, that we have got the wrong Bible. They would seek to introduce you to their translation, in which they have got "Jehovah" in place of our word "LORD". To that degree they are probably nearer to the original, though they are not there. The Jerusalem Bible is a very fine Roman Catholic translation. They have said "YHWH" instead of "LORD." Wherever in the Old Testament you see the word "LORD" in capital letters, that is where the name of God was, and if they could spell it, it would be there. So they have gone back to "YHWH". I notice in Moffatt's translation "The Eternal" is used, to try to get across this sense of *being*. Even if all our Bibles did put "Jehovah" or "YHWH" or "The Eternal" in, I still don't think we would use that name. Why not? Because God has a different name. Because when we exalt his name, we don't use that name at all. That's not how we think of it. When we say, "Hallowed be thy name," we never think of this. Oh we might sing, "Guide me, O thou great Jehovah," but that is because we are seeing the Christian life in Old Testament terms, and so we use their name for him as they went through the wilderness. But we are not tying ourselves to the name. We might sing: "The God of Abraham Praise" but again we are just going back to the Hebrews' name. We are not feeling that we are tied to it.

What, then, is God's name? Two things will explain this. The first is: *Jesus called God "Father"*. And he said: **When you pray, say "Father".** He did not say: "When you pray, say Jehovah." That is the first big change you notice when you step into the New Testament. The new name or the new title that is being used in prayer is "Father". Jesus used it and he told his followers to use it. He had not been brought up to do so. This was something new that Jesus introduced.

The Jews would never have dared to call God "Dad". They didn't even dare to say his name, never mind be as intimate with the Almighty as that. The unique Christian prayer begins, "Our Father, which art in heaven; hallowed be thy name." So the first thing that the name of God means to us is Father.

There is a deeper reason still why we don't use "Jehovah": not only did Jesus call God "Father" but — and this is what I try to say to every JW who comes to me — Jesus called himself Jehovah. That is the most extraordinary thing in the New Testament to me. Now where do I find that — because the word "Jehovah" isn't in the New Testament? I told the last Jehovah's Witness to visit me, "You come back to me when you can point out the word 'Jehovah' to me in the New Testament, because that's where I live—in the New Testament as the fulfilment of the Old."

Well he came back before he had found it. I said, "You

come back when you've found it." He came back but it is
not there. So why do I dare to say that Jesus called himself
Jehovah? Seven times Jesus said "I Am" and added a
description. "I am the Light of the World"; "I am the
Bread of Heaven"; "I am the Good Shepherd"; "I am the
Resurrection and the Life"; "I am the Way, the Truth, and
the Life"; "I am the True Vine." You may not have noticed,
but every time he said it in the hearing of the Jews, they
immediately tried to kill him for it.

Why did they try to kill Jesus every time he said those
words? The answer comes across in the English; even more
so in the Greek. He used a particular expression which isn't
just simply "I Am" but is better translated, "I, I Am." If you
are interested in Greek; *ego, eimi*. Well, *eimi* means "I am"
and *ego* means "I," and he said, "I, I Am." Then he did
precisely what YHWH did in the Old Testament—told them
what it meant. "I, I Am" —What am I? "I am the Bread of
Heaven" —and they got the message. There is no doubt about
it that the Jews realised he was saying "YHWH, I Am", and
then filling out the word as his Father had done in the Old
Testament. It was for this reason that they crucified Jesus,
no other. It was for this reason that the Jews said, "He must
be done to death." It was for this reason, whatever political
charges they managed to produce at the trial.

There are three occasions on which Jesus used the phrase
"I Am" without even saying anything after it, which made
it perfectly clear.

One day Jesus said—in colloquial language, I am para-
phrasing: "I was talking with Abraham the other day", and
they said, "You are not yet fifty years old. How do you know
Abraham?" Jesus said, "Verily, verily..." and in his language
that is, "Amen, amen" [truly, truly; certainly, certainly] I say
to you, before Abraham was, I, I Am." Do you know what
the next verse says? They took up stones to stone him. They

got the message. "I am YHWH. I have always been. I am the Eternal One. I Am that I Am. That's how I knew Abraham."

The second occasion was in the garden of Gethsemane. Jesus was there praying, and there came soldiers from the temple to arrest him. Notice they were temple soldiers, Jewish soldiers, not Romans. They came to arrest him and he said, "Who are you looking for?" They said, "Jesus of Nazareth," and he replied, "I, I Am," and literally they fell backward on the ground. It says that. Now why? Why should they fall on the ground? The answer is they expected him to be struck dead for saying it; the blasphemy of it! So they finally took him away in chains when they saw that nothing happened to him and of course, nothing would—it was true!

They took him to his trial before Annas and Caiaphas and they couldn't get the witnesses to agree. They couldn't get the evidence, so finally the judge, quite illegally, asked the prisoner a leading question and said, "Tell us, I adjure you by the living God," which means you must answer, "Are you the Son of God?" Jesus said, "I, I Am." The high priest tore his clothes and said, "You've heard him. We don't need witnesses. Here's a man who stands self-condemned for blasphemy. He calls himself Jehovah." That is what the trial was all about and then it was just a matter of finding a charge that Pilate would accept. So the real reason why Jesus was crucified was that he called himself Jehovah. I wish the Jehovah's Witnesses could grasp that simple point. I hope that you grasp it, because it means now the name is the name *Jesus*. It means that now when you go out to witness, you don't go on the words of Isaiah, "You shall be my witnesses, says Jehovah." You go by the words of Acts 1:8, "You shall receive power," said Jesus, "and you will be witnesses to me." They went everywhere. They didn't preach Jehovah, they preached Jesus —but in preaching Jesus they were preaching Jehovah. Jesus is the name in which they baptised people, and one of the interesting things which is thought to be a discrepancy in the New Testament is not. Jesus said, "Go and baptise people in the name" [singular] — "the name of Father, Son, and Spirit." What name did they use when they fulfilled that command? You will find in every case in the New Testament they only baptised into the name of Jesus. Why? Because the name of the Father was Jesus; The Father is the Father of Jesus. The name of the Son—Jesus; the name of the Spirit—the Spirit of Jesus, and one name covers all now.

This is the new name. It was in this name that they healed people. Here was a man who had been lame for forty years and Peter said, "If you want to know the power by which we healed this man, let it be known. It was not by our power, it was the power of the name of Jesus of Nazareth." You hallow the name of God when you hallow the name of Jesus. You are witnesses to Jehovah when you speak to the world about Jesus Christ. God now has a Christian name, and we have been given the privilege of calling him by it.

6

PEACE; QUIET

In Chapters 1–2 of Isaiah, the prophet was speaking to a nation that had won a war and lost the peace, a nation that had allowed injustice and unrighteous things to come in, and was therefore inviting war again. Having prophesied to the nation, there is then a prediction for the future:

In the last days, it will come to pass that the mountain of the Lord shall tower above all peaks, lifted high above the hills, and all the nations shall swarm to it. Many peoples will arrive and say, "Come, let us go up to the mountain of the Lord and to the house of the God of Jacob. He will teach us and give us knowledge of his ways, and we will follow in his paths." For the law goes forth from Zion, and the word of the Lord from Jerusalem and he will judge between the nations and make decisions between the peoples. Then they shall hammer their swords into ploughshares, and their spears into pruning hooks. Nation shall lift no sword against nation, and never again will they learn to make war.

That tells you how to keep the peace. It tells you that you cannot have peace without justice and righteousness, and that as long as there is evil in the world we need to make our swords. But when he comes back again, then we shall turn them into ploughshares. I want to take the next three letters of the alphabet: "O, P, and Q. I want to begin with the middle letter, because it's the peak of these three letters—*peace*; the peace of God; the God of peace. These are phrases from the scriptures. Two texts come to mind, one from the book of Isaiah: "Thou dost keep him in perfect peace whose mind is stayed on thee"; and from the second letter to the Thessalonians: "Now the Lord of peace himself give you peace always."

We get very cynical about the word "peace". When we look at the world in which we live, we cannot say that we got peace as a result of the two world wars. Now I want to ask what it means when both the Old and the New Testament call God "The God of peace". Should we be among the cynics who say: "God of peace? In two thousand years since Jesus came to this earth we have had nothing but wars — we don't believe there is a God of peace, otherwise why should there be such a world of strife and war and bloodshed?"

What does the word mean? I want to take the three languages that were written above the cross—Latin, Greek, and Hebrew, and look at the word "peace" in each. We shall discover that in fact the word "peace" means different things to different people. It meant one thing to the Romans, another thing to the Greeks, and another to the Hebrews.

Take the Roman word "peace": *pax*; *pacis*, from which we get our word "pact". It was a political word and means quite simply the absence of war. In the days of the New Testament they enjoyed what was called the *Pax Romana*. Throughout the then known world there was peace, and had there not been the Roman army there would not have been peace. It was because of that political peace that the gospel could spread so quickly and jump from place to place without any passports and controls, and the gospel could be spread.

I have the feeling that that is the kind of peace my generation prayed for when, during the second world war, our churches were full on national days of prayer. But I do not believe that God is that kind of God. If we hope for political peace in our time then we shall be terribly disappointed, because Jesus said that until the end of history, until the day he came back, there would be wars and rumours of wars. Therefore, those who know the words of Jesus and who have steeped their minds in what he thought about the world will not be shaken when World War III starts. Only those who have a naïve view of both Jesus and God the Father will be shaken in their faith.

Jesus also said, "...but let not your hearts be troubled." He will come again to deal with the situation. We hope that our children may have a measure of peace, and that there may be periods of peace in the world, but we know perfectly well that there will be "wars and rumours of wars" because the last world wars of the twentieth century did not deal with the cause of war.

The Greek word for peace is *eirene*, hence the girl's name Irene. Parents may choose that name hoping that they will grow up to be placid people. It is a difficult and dangerous thing to do as I have mentioned, to name your children before they have grown up! (If you happen to be an "Irene", of course, you may be very peaceful and placid.) The Greeks interpreted peace, *eirene*, as being the absence—note again it is negative, the absence of *inward* conflict. For them it was not an outward thing, it was an inward thing, and if you were free of inward conflict, then you had peace. From this word comes our word "eirenical". Have you heard somebody described in a discussion group as an "eirenical" person, someone who pours oil on conflict and takes the disturbance out of the discussion — an eirenical spirit?

The Greeks' favourite idea was *ataraxia*, which means

tranquillity. This suggests someone who is not easily upset, who doesn't get disturbed, doesn't get too close to people so that he doesn't get tied up emotionally with them, and doesn't get too emotionally involved even in his own problems. He stays on an even keel; he has this kind of peace. It is almost a cultivated indifference and independence of others.

I am not like that myself, but I know many people like this who seem to have a kind of cultivated serenity and never seem to get upset or excited and just keep on an even keel all their life. You feel that if you meet them in ten years' time they will still be on that smooth course. I envy such people. My life has never been as placid as that, but is that the peace of God, or is it a temperamental thing? Is it something you are born with?

Now let us look at the Hebrew word for peace: *shalom*. It is a tremendous thrill to step off the plane in Israel and be greeted by your bus or taxi driver, "Shalom". It is so much nicer than hello, or even goodbye, which is a contraction of, "God be with ye". Shalom is a lovely greeting you hear everywhere in Israel. It is the same as I heard from the Arabs when they said, "Salaam". We don't use any word like it in this country.

What does this Hebrew word *shalom* for peace mean? It means something quite positive. It is neither the absence of outward conflict nor the absence of inward conflict. It is the presence of two things. Physically, it is the *presence of health*, and that of course is a very great blessing of peace, so when you say "Shalom" to someone you are saying: "Good health to you." But you are saying more than that. It is not just the presence of health, it is the *presence of harmony*, which means that you are in the *right relationship with other people and with your God.* As parents we found that sometimes we could get peace in our house by sending each of our children to a different room. "Go to your separate bedrooms!" That was very rarely needed, fortunately. We can get "Roman peace" like that; we can get maybe "Greek peace" for ourselves like that, but we cannot get "shalom" like that. We get shalom when we go for a walk through the countryside together as a family and we are in harmony with ourselves, with nature, and with God. It is something utterly positive. It is not just the absence — "leave me alone in peace"; "get other people out of my home and out of my sight"; "if only I didn't have to work for my boss I could be placid." Have you heard that kind of talk? No, it is: "give me harmony with my boss, with my family, with my awkward neighbour, with my God."

God is described again and again in scripture as the "God of peace". *You will never get the peace of God until you find the God of peace*. You notice again and again in scripture, if you are offered the peace of God at the end of a letter, you will find the God of peace mentioned near the beginning.

Let us look first at the God of peace. Why is he described as the God of peace? Precisely because he is the God of perfect harmony. There is a harmony, which is threefold, and I give you just little glimpses of the harmony in God.

First of all, there is a harmony in what he says. God never contradicts himself. I went through a naughty stage as a young man where I thought the Bible was full of contradictions. I think we all go through that stage. I thought I could pick holes in the book and I could show where it seemingly contradicted this, that, and the other. I started with a very long list. It has rapidly reduced over the years as I have studied my Bible more deeply. I discovered that this book, written over fourteen hundred years by over forty different authors in three different languages — none of the authors knowing that they were writing part of the Bible or even knowing what other parts would be written — agrees with itself from cover to cover; that there is a harmony of teaching so that it does not matter what chapter you study, you will find the same truths as you find elsewhere in it—the harmony in what God says—God is a God of peace.

The harmony in what God does in our history seems to be utter chaos, doesn't it—at first sight? But those who know the God of peace can see that God is moving the whole of history, every event in it, towards one grand, far-off divine event to which the whole creation moves, namely, the consummation of everything in Christ. You can see this happening.

It is the unbeliever who says, "I can see no sense in it all." It is the unbeliever who can't see the events drawing nearer which mean that "we can look up, for the day of our redemption draws nigh." The Christian can see a harmony in history. The Christian can see that evil dictators are allowed so far by God and then struck and stopped. God gives mankind a lot of rope but not enough to hang themselves. You can see God's restraining hand again and again, allowing evil to teach men their lesson, but never allowing men's evil to destroy the world.

I am not afraid that the world will be destroyed by atomic bombs. It will not be. Man may destroy a bit of society, but he won't be able to end history. God said that is in his hands, and there is a harmony of history in what God has done that is all leading to the climax of the pattern.

What is true beauty? True beauty is proportion—when you study the Greek statues of human beings, you discover that they are beautiful because they got everything in perfect proportion. One part of your body out of proportion spoils the beauty. The same is true not just of physical beauty but of moral beauty, of character. Get one virtue out of proportion and you destroy beauty of character. If someone gets their love out of proportion, they destroy the beauty of their character. The same is true of righteous indignation. But when you begin to look at the character of God, what a harmony there is in what he is. We have thought of his *holiness*, his *indignation* and his *justice*; his *kindness*, his *love* and his *mercy*, and of his *fatherly goodness* and *almighty power*. We are thinking now of his *peace* and it all blends perfectly. Do you notice there is not one thing out of proportion? Not one thing out of balance — God's attributes are in perfect harmony. God is Father, Son and Holy Spirit, and there is perfect harmony between those three persons of the godhead, so if you were to ask one of those three for his opinion on something, you would get the same truth.

Jesus prayed that his disciples ("those whom you gave me...") would be in the same kind of harmony with each other as he has with his Father: "...so that they may be one as we are one" —so we think the same way, say the same things and have the same attitude. That is the kind of harmony he was praying for. It wasn't an organisational unity. It was a harmony such that whatever church you go to you hear the same gospel, meet the same Jesus Christ, and the same power of God unto salvation will be yours. The harmony between Jesus and the Father was real and showed in everything Jesus did; and a harmony between Christians should show in everything we do.

We turn briefly to *the peace of God*. This harmony that God has within himself he wants to give to people. That is why in the New Testament it is stated that Jesus came to bring peace. He was called the Prince of Peace. When he was born it was said: "Glory to God in the highest, and on earth peace...." The cynic says it has been a dismal failure. We have had war ever since. I say to that cynic: you haven't read that word as it ought to be read. Jesus has brought peace on earth and *you* don't know it. "... and on earth peace."

When Jesus died, he had no money to leave. He had nothing to leave except one thing, and so the night before he died, he said this to his friends: I am going to leave something to you—*my peace I leave*.... Not as the world gives, not that kind of peace. He deliberately made it utterly clear that they would not know the kind of outer peace that the world tries to get and to give. The first word he uttered when he came back from the grave was this: "Peace be unto you." You can have it now, because you can't have someone's legacy until they have died.

They went forth in his name to preach peace—peace that could bring Jew and Gentile together; peace that could bring bond and free together; peace that could bring male and female together; peace that could bring cultured Greek and uncultured barbarian together. This was the gospel of peace, and when I pick up their letters this is the kind of benediction I find again and again. "And the peace of God which passes all understanding will keep your hearts and minds in Christ Jesus." Here is another: "Now the Lord of peace himself give you peace always, by all means." Here's another, "And let the peace of God rule in your hearts."

What does it mean? I am going to go to the other two letters now. God is a God of peace. Why? Because he is a God of Order—what does it result in? *Q*uietness, and we are thinking now about the order, the peace, and the quiet of God. Because he is a God of order, he is a God of peace; and because he is a God of peace, he is a God who can speak with a still, small voice and make you *quiet*. Let us apply this very practically as the Bible does. In down to earth terms, what difference would it make to us if *the God of peace* gives us *the peace of God*?

Two differences. In our life together as a church, we should be ordered. I am quoting now from 1 Corinthians 14 where there was a church that became very disordered. They began to exercise gifts, not in an orderly manner (and there is nothing wrong with gifts of the Spirit being exercised in church in an orderly manner) but in a *disorderly* manner.

People were speaking more than one at a time. They were getting up and creating a disturbance; they were making a noise, and Paul says: God is a God of order, of peace, not a God of confusion, so that your church life ought to be ordered. That will tell the world that you worship a God of peace.

Think about somebody coming into your assembly and you are all shouting at once and doing different things and paying no attention to each other. Now I know there are different ways of ordering your worship, and I don't really mind which order you have if it is real and in the Spirit. I don't mind if you have no order in the sense of writing it down beforehand, as long as it is ordered. I can worship with the joyful praise of the Salvation Army. I like the liturgy of the Church of England; I like Baptist worship, but whatever form it takes—Pentecostal, Brethren, whatever — God is a God of peace, and therefore our worship is to be ordered.

It will tell people, "We do not bring you here to confuse you. We do not bring you here to disturb you. We bring you here to a God of order who will order your lives. The God whose Spirit breathed over the chaos of creation, and brought order out of it, can breathe over the chaos of your lives and bring order out of your daily life." That is why we have ordered worship, because God is a God of order and not confusion. As far as your private, individual life goes, the other thing the Bible does say is that if you really get the peace of God, not only will Christian worship and witness together be ordered and not chaotic and confused, your individual life will be quiet. Christians are not noisy people. "In quietness and confidence shall be your strength." The effect of righteousness, as Isaiah taught, will be peace, and the result of righteousness will be quietness and trust forever. Have you noticed that the people who really know the peace of God are quiet people? Of course they are. They may raise their voice as Jesus did when he turned evil out of the temple, but they are quiet people. Paul tells us to live quietly. How different this is to the world's noise and chatter. We are told in the Bible to live quietly, the God of peace will be with us.

I was with a group staying in a hotel who spent a quarter of an hour in complete silence. We each went to our room, alone with God. I went through to the kitchen on my way upstairs after this, and the staff said, "What on earth's the matter with them all?" They were absolutely shattered and the other hotel guests said, "Where have they gone?" The whole place was as quiet as the grave. But in that fifteen-minute silence God said more to us I think than in the rest of the time at the event. "Be still and know that I am God." God speaks.

How does this work out? First a word to men. Here is a text for you: "Aspire to live quietly; mind your own business. Work in quietness and earn your own living." That is practical, isn't it? Get on with your job quietly, and I'll tell you this—every employer values an employee who will do that and quietly get on with their job.

Women, are you interested in beauty? Here is the Bible's advice on how to be beautiful: "Let not yours be the outward adorning with braiding of hair, decoration of gold and wearing of robes; but let it be that of your inner self, the imperishable beauty of a quiet and gentle spirit, which in God's sight is very precious." Do you want to be a beautiful woman? Then a quiet and a gentle spirit — the peace of God — will do that for you. The peace of God will be with you.

7

REIGN; SOVEREIGNTY

Consider Psalm 103, "The Lord has established his throne in the heavens and his kingdom ruleth over all." And from Revelation 19, "Hallelujah! For the Lord God omnipotent reigneth. Let us rejoice and exalt and give him glory." These are texts from the Old and the New Testament saying the same thing—that *God is King*.

He is described as the only potentate, the King of kings and the Lord of lords. The Bible begins in the throne room of God and it ends in the throne room of God and, in between, human thrones and human empires come and go, human kingdoms and powers and glories wax and wane —but throughout it all the throne of God is established in the heavens. This is such a big theme that I feel utterly inadequate to try and get it across to you, but if I can convey something of the sense of the majesty of our mighty God then we have filled out the picture a little more. "O magnify the Lord with me." The note that needs to be added to many people's confession is the majesty of God as King.

Before ever Jesus taught us to call God "Father" he came into Galilee preaching the kingdom, the kingship, the royalty of God, and the absence of this note is the explanation of why much of our worship gets a little too "pally" and a little too earthly, and hasn't a lot of that sense of awe and reverence, such as you would certainly have if you were going to have

THE CHARACTER OF GOD

an audience with Her Majesty Queen Elizabeth II. We meet for an audience with his majesty the King of kings.

It is very difficult in these modern days to get across the meaning of the word "king". For one thing many royal families have come to an end. At least twenty-four thrones of Europe have tumbled into the dust, and many crowns have fallen off royal heads. Even in countries that still have royal families, such as our own, royalty no longer *rules*. Royalty has become a constitutional monarchy, a figurehead, and bless her, the one person who can't do her own will in this land seems to be her majesty, the Queen. She is regarded as the servant of all and must do whatever the nation wishes her to do, but in the olden days and still in certain parts of the world, a kingdom isn't defined in terms of territory but of dominion. Step over that boundary and you are in the kingdom of a chief or king, under *his* dominion. He rules, and within that territory his word is law and his will is absolute. In the days when the Bible was written, the word "king" had this note of absolute dominion and authority, and to call someone King of kings was to say something very big indeed.

So we must exercise our imagination and get back into the days when "kingdom" and "king" meant something great — a powerful dominion — and referred to a person who had absolute control of all that happened within his dominions, and that is the *reign* or the *sovereignty of God*. I prefer those words to the word "kingdom". For "kingdom" nowadays simply means a geographical territory. When Christ came preaching the kingdom of God, the kingdom of heaven, he was preaching the reign of God, the sovereignty of God, the absolute dominion of Almighty God over all that he has made. In other words, if you want to sum up my message in one sentence and if you forget everything else, remember this: "God is still on the throne." That was a song title, and a little girl mistook it for "God is on the phone"! And it is true that there can be prayer communication between him and us. But it is also true to say the prayer life of some is not praying to "God on the throne" but a "God on the phone" in the sense of someone they can just ring up and get through to and say, "Will you do what *I* want straight away — here's an emergency, put it right." But when you approach our God who is *on the throne* you approach him in a rather different spirit to someone on the phone. You approach him with reverence and awe. You don't try to persuade him to do your will, you say, "What is *your* will?" —and then you seek to do it.

Human reason would never tell you that God was on the throne. I am telling you something that the greatest brain in the world couldn't tell you. This is something mankind would never have discovered if God had not told us this in his Word. For wherever you look you find almost a complete absence of any evidence that would suggest that God is still on the throne.

Think of the world of nature. You watch the weather forecast for tomorrow and you might ask: "Is God on the throne? Does he really control the weather?" It may seem as if nature is bound with iron laws and somehow even if God created the world he must have left it running on its own many centuries ago, as if he made a watch and wound it up and just left it ticking. You would not come to the conclusion that God was on the throne by looking at nature. Sometimes nature does things that would suggest that God is not in control of it. A typhoon, hurricane or earthquake occurs, you see the pictures in the media, and say, "God on the throne? You tell me that God is in control and that happens?" (See my book *Why Does God Allow Natural Disasters?* for a discussion of this.)

Human reason would not find this truth in nature. Nor

would human reason alone be likely to find this in *history*. We see the horror of wars, so people say to me: "God in control, letting things like that happen? You try and tell me that God is on the throne and that history is in his hands. I don't believe it, I can't see the evidence."

Nor does human reason find the throne of God in human *experience*. "You're going to tell me that God is on the throne and in control when that happened to my child? You're going to tell me that God is in control? I don't believe it. I think we're at the mercy of sheer chance; we're at the mercy of microbes so small we cannot see them. We're not under the control of an omnipotent God."

So, wherever you look, people say, "I cannot see this" —and of course you can't. This is not a truth that human reason can see. You would never know that God is on the throne if you were left to your own reason.

I find this truth however in the Bible, the book of *divine* revelation, and therefore every one of us must decide whether we are going to accept human reason or divine revelation as authoritative. Whether you think we are subject to chaos, chance or the blind laws of some mechanical universe — or whether you will believe that God has everything in his control. Which are you going to accept?

Let us look at what the Bible says about God's sovereignty, his control, his omnipotence, then ask whether it could be true. The Bible is about God's will being done and the fact that nothing can thwart his will — that, his being on the throne of the universe, everything he says *happens*, and the Bible begins and ends with his decrees.

First, the Old Testament and we begin with nature which I have already mentioned. We begin in the throne room of God in Genesis 1, and God makes a decree, "Let there be light", and there was light.

Notice that in Revelation 4 it says: "Thou art worthy

O Lord to receive glory and honour and power. For Thou didst create all things and by Thy will they existed and were created." God was sovereign in creation and what he decreed happened. "He spoke and it was done," said the Psalmist. That is the sovereignty of God.

Having *created* the word of nature, did God continue to *control* it? Is it really in his hands? The Bible unanimously states that it is. Let's take the weather for example. People say "What's the point of praying about the weather? The weather is subject to the meteorological laws and to what seems chance—and the smiling announcer on the television screen apologises that they were wrong yesterday and that it poured instead of being sunny! Is God in control of the weather?

Well, listen to the Bible: "Whatever the Lord pleases, he does in heaven and on earth, in the seas and all deeps. He sends the clouds, the lightning, the rain, the wind."

Read the Bible and you will find that God again and again used the weather for his purposes. Consider Noah, God caused it to rain. There was an order from the throne of God and the rain washed away an evil society. God sent a great east wind and split the Red Sea in two, and a nation was saved from destruction. The order to the wind came from the throne. God sent the hail on Egypt, such hail as never was before, but there was one small patch of Egypt on which not one hailstone fell — the land of Goshen where his people were. God can cause the sun to stand still for a battle, and hold the stars in their courses. Now this is the biblical picture of God, and it goes right through to the Son of God standing in the stern of a boat and saying to the wind and the waves "Get down, be quiet" and there was a great calm; the sovereignty of God over the weather.

Does God control the animals? Consider this: "For every beast of the field of the forest is mine, the cattle on a thousand hills, and all the birds of the air, and all that moves in the field is mine." That is the word of God. He can tell the flies what to do, for he told the flies to go to Egypt and they went. He told the locusts what to do, and they went. He told the ravens to feed a man named Elijah and they did. Many people think the whale is the big difficulty in Jonah, but I can tell you the worm is just as big a difficulty. The whale and the worm both did what God told them to do. You get it again when Jesus got on a colt, the foal of an ass. I recommend you to try riding one of those on which man has never yet sat. You wouldn't stay on ten seconds, yet Jesus controlled that beast all the way into the city.

Both nature and animals are perfectly under the sovereignty of God —and, asked, can be used to speak. Two cattle pulling the ark of the Covenant can know which way Jerusalem is, and where they ought to take the ark, and the Philistines stand amazed that even cows know the will of God. That is the picture of God in the Bible: everything under his sovereign will.

Now let's turn to history. Back to the Jews. You cannot explain Jewish history except in terms of God's sovereign control. By every human factor the Jews ought to have gone out of existence three thousand years ago, yet they are still there. By every human explanation they should never even have got through the Old Testament period, yet they did. Why? Because, as Isaiah and Jeremiah say, the relationship between Israel and God was that between a potter and clay, and whatever happened to them was simply the hand of the potter shaping their destiny. He could break them, and make them, and mould them, but he was God and they were the clay in the potter's hands. Therefore whatever he decided for them came to pass. If he decided they should be in their own land — they were. If he decided they shouldn't be, then they weren't — and no-one could stop it.

As Isaiah says, "God creates good and evil", not meaning moral evil but physical suffering. God creates both, and when God sent the wind and rain from the Mediterranean it rained and the land had food. When God reversed the weather and the east wind came from the Arabian Desert, they had a famine —and God could change it at will. Their history reveals his perfect control of the nation, but if we think it was limited to the Jews then we have too narrow of a view of God. Read the Old Testament again and you find that God has the nations in the hollow of his hand, not just the Jews, and that he moves them as easily as you or I could move a piece on the chessboard. He says, "I brought the Philistines from Caphtor. I brought the Syrians from Kir", and he moves the nations around according to his purpose. One of the greatest demonstrations of that would be when the Jews were in captivity, away in the land of Babylon. How were they ever going to be set free? How could they ever get back to their own land? Isaiah says: Cyrus my anointed is coming to take over that kingdom and he'll set you free and let you go back. God moved a whole empire up against the captors of Israel and set them free from the nations. Get this big view of God — a God who can control all nature and all history — but you won't get it anywhere except the Bible. Then you can consider daily news and you can see that the nations are in his hands.

Let us come down to the personal level of human experience. In the Bible you can find God's sovereignty there. The book of Proverbs says: "A man's mind plans his way but the Lord directs his steps." You are going to make your plans but don't think you can thwart his plans. Someone's mind may make decisions, but his steps are directed by God and he may never know it, or he may know it like Joseph. It seemed as if one tragedy after another hit that poor man. Sold by his brothers into slavery, wrongly accused by Potiphar of meddling with his wife, he had been thrown into prison and forgotten in his cell. Yet when Joseph's brothers came to Egypt he said that the Lord planned this. Joseph knew they had meant to harm him, but it was the plan of the Lord, so that he would be there in Egypt in a position to feed them when they were hungry. Joseph could see the sovereignty of God worked out in his life.

Consider Job. He didn't understand what was going on. He only knew that he lost all his business and all his money and that all his children were killed in a disaster, then finally he was himself stricken with a deadly disease. What was Job's reaction to that? He didn't understand why it had happened. He didn't know that God had permitted it. But what did he say when he lost every one of his children? "The Lord gave and the Lord hath taken away." That was a big enough thing to say, but he went on to say: "Blessed be the name of the Lord." I would say there is hardly one funeral in fifty at which you can really say that to express the deepest feelings of those who are there. It almost seems hypocrisy when we are asking: "Why; why?" I thank him even for giving me those children for such a short while. Blessed be his name.... You don't often find that attitude.

Then, when Job was stricken down in health, his wife had the typical attitude of the unbeliever and said, "Look what he has done to you, curse him and die." He said quietly, "We have received good from the hand of the Lord and shall we not receive evil?" Are we going to dictate to God what sort of a life he sends us? Oh, what marvellous acceptance of the sovereignty of God.

Take now an example of a man who was used not for good but for evil — Pharaoh. Pharaoh is the outstanding example in the scriptures of a man whom God in his sovereign power used as a demonstration of his judgment. It says that Pharaoh's heart was hardened by God. Quoting that in

Romans 9, Paul adds this comment: "The Lord will have mercy on whom he will have mercy and will harden whoever he will harden. Who are you to say to the potter 'I don't like the way you're making that clay.'" That is New Testament.

Has God not a right to do that to Pharaoh? Has he not a right to harden whom he will and have mercy on whom he will? Have we forgotten that he is God, that we should tell him what to do? So we find in that great prayer in 1 Chronicles: "Thine O Lord is the greatness and the power and the glory and the victory and the majesty, for all that is in heaven and in the earth is Thine. Thine is the kingdom."

Do you notice — kingdom, power, and glory? Words in the Lord's prayer, there they are in the Old Testament. "Our God is in the heavens," said the Psalmist. He does whatever he pleases; that is God.

In the New Testament first of all you see the Almighty sovereignty of God in Christ. Why Mary? You will find no answer to that question, any more than you find an answer to the question: why the Jews? The answer isn't in the Jews, it is in the sovereign will of God; the answer isn't in Mary, it is in the sovereign will of God.

"Mary, you're going to have a boy," and Mary said, "Behold the handmaid of the Lord. Be it unto me according to Thy word." All the foul gossip that was going to go around about this unmarried woman, and still is going on in the Middle East. Yet Jesus was born by the omnipotent will of God, who decided who would be the mother, where he should be born, when he should be born. It was by royal decree from the throne of heaven.

You find it all through our Lord's ministry. You find that he came to do the will of his Father God. The sovereignty over wind and waves was the same sovereignty that he exercised over the disciples, and he said, "You didn't choose me, I chose you...." The twelve disciples were not twelve men who chose Jesus, they were twelve men whom Jesus chose. In his prayer in John 17, Jesus thanks the Father for giving him those twelve men, "You have given them to me." It is so different from talking about "deciding to follow Jesus".

Take the Lord's Prayer, the model prayer, "Thy will be done ... for thine is the kingdom." The Son of God who taught us that is the Son of God who practised it.

Come with me now to two moments of prayer in the earthly life of Jesus. When the disciples returned and said "Even the demons are subject to us in your name" he rejoiced, he exulted in Spirit and said, "I rejoice that you have hidden these things from the wise and revealed them to babes and sucklings; even so Father ... for it seemed good in thy sight." Whatever seemed good in his Father's sight, Jesus rejoiced in it.

When he came to that agony in Gethsemane, he prayed, "Father if thou be willing take this cup away ... nevertheless not my will but thy will be done." You know, when those evil men decided to nail him on the cross, they thought it was their decision. Pilate thought that he had decided to hand him over. Annas and Caiaphas thought that they had decided to get him crucified. The people thought that they had decided by shouting, "Crucify him!" But who really decided that Christ should die on the cross? — The Father.

When Peter preached his first sermon he said: "This Jesus, delivered up according to the definite plan and foreknowledge of God ... You crucified." The cross was not men's plan, it was God's. If somebody says, "Well I just can't understand this" —well, don't try to, just accept what God has said.

There are those who deny human responsibility, and they cut out some of the Bible. There are those who deny divine sovereignty and they too have to cut out some of the Bible. I only know that whereas wicked men decided to put Jesus to death it was all according to God's predetermined plan. Ask me to explain it and I answer, "I'm not God. I'm only telling you what God says." This is why the Lamb of God was slain from the foundation of the world. The cross was no tragic afterthought, it was in God's mind, way before the world began — from the foundation of the world that Lamb was slain for the sins of men.

Now come to Christians. In the New Testament, God's sovereignty is wonderfully demonstrated in the Christian life. Someone wrote: "When you come to the gate of salvation you find written on the outside, 'whosoever will may come', but when you get inside and turn around and look back you'll see something else written on the door: "Elect according to the foreknowledge of God." This is not a truth for sinners but for saints, and it is the most precious truth that you discover — that in fact though you thought at the time that you chose God, you now look back and you see: "God chose me ... in him before the foundation of the world." It means that your salvation rests not on you but on him. It means that in his grace and mercy he laid his hand on you. Paul couldn't get over this and in letter after letter that he wrote it comes out: "God's elect...."

It is a most precious truth that holds a Christian in days of despair and depression: that God chose me in Christ before the foundation of the world. It comes out again and again. In Acts 13 it says that Paul went to a certain town and preached, and then: "As many as were ordained to eternal life believed." It begins with God's decision, not man's. It begins in the heart of God's plan.

In Romans 8 you get the same sort of thing as Paul says: "Those whom he predestined, he also called. Those whom he called he also justified and those whom he justified he also sanctified, glorified" — but it began in God's will not ours. It continues in his providential care. It is wonderful to the Christian, to know this – Romans 8:28, "We know that in everything God works for good with those who love him and who are called according to his purpose." This is not an overall fatalism saying whatever will be, will be; Oh well, I'm sure it's all for the best....

A saint can know that whatever happens, whatever tragedy may strike tomorrow, whatever difficulty he may run into, God will work for his good because he is called according to the purpose of God. It is in this that a Christian's final security lies. If it is God's will to call out a people for his own name and to take them at last to heaven, who can defeat that will? If it is his will that none shall pluck us out of his hand, who can do so? Our security is in God's sovereignty.

You can see that in this matter human reason and divine revelation are contradictory, and you must choose between them. *Human reason* says that human responsibility is the last word or else we are just pushed around by fate or some other impersonal chance. *Divine revelation says that God is still on the throne*.

You get a different reaction to this truth from a saint and a sinner. You can find out which you are talking to by the reaction they have. A sinner greets this with sullen rebellion, a saint greets it with sweet rejoicing. It stabs a sinner's pride; it stimulates a saint's praise. It fills a sinner full of questions. It fills a saint full of peace. The sinner will say, "Well, if God has predestined everything, what's the point of praying?" What does he think prayer is, to make God do *my* will? That is probably what he does think, but prayer is surely to do the will of God.

God is on the throne, his will is going to be done, his kingdom is sure to come, and this makes us all the more earnest in prayer. We don't say, "Oh well, if that's so then it's alright, we needn't pray for anything." No, we are here to do the will of God. He has instructed us pray. We are told in 1

John 5 that if we ask anything according to *his* will, he hears us. Not what *we* will, but what *he* wills; so that is what we ask for in prayer. Too much of our prayer is for what *we* will. When you preach this and say that "God is on the throne," some will say: "Well what's the point of preaching? If God has predestined, if God decides and elects, why preach?" I answer, "What do you think preaching is? Do you think preaching is me trying to impose my will on you and on your will? I am preaching to do the will of God — believing I am to preach according to the will of God; believing that that same will would use my word to do what he wants to do, and will touch some hearts, and will bring hearers nearer to the Lord, and to an understanding of *his* holy will.

So the saint does not rebel against this. He finds in it two things. First of all, it produces the right kind of submission to God in the saint. Mary is the good example, as I have already quoted: "Be it unto me according to Thy will," but also what about David? When his life was in peril he said, "Lord, I'd like to get back to the palace and to be out of this danger but let him do to me as seemeth good unto him."

This is the answer to grumbling and complaining. This is the answer to fretting and rebellion — to accept God's will. Not in a spirit of fatalistic indifference, not in a spirit of, "Oh well, I don't need to do anything," but in a spirit of, "Thy will be done" with the emphasis on the "done". It is fatalism that simply sits still and says, "Whatever will be, will be," but that is quite different from saying: your will be done. I want to do your will. I want to be active in your will, knowing that in your will is my peace.

Finally, the saint finds here that which provides security. God has the whole world in his hand. To go to bed at night knowing that he has got the whole world in his hand, that is security: I will not fear what man can do to me. In your will is my peace.

God's plan cannot miscarry, his purpose cannot fail, and his kingdom cannot be thwarted, and in that is our security. God is still on the throne. I am sure your mind is full of questions; mine is. For human reason doesn't find this palatable. At the end of Romans 11, after three chapters discussing the sovereignty of God, Paul writes: "Oh the depth of the riches of the wisdom and the knowledge of God. How unsearchable are his judgments and his ways are past finding out." One day I know that I shall understand that his will has always been right and best.

8

TRINITY; UNITY

In 2 Corinthians 13:14 are words which you must have heard many times: "The grace of the Lord Jesus Christ and the love of God and the fellowship of the Holy Spirit be with you all."

If we think about those whom we feel are "great" human beings, we sometimes find, when we read about their lives, that they are complex in character. Almighty God is not "complex" in the way a human being may be complex. But God is infinitely great, and he has revealed much about himself in his Word, and it is impossible in a few simple thoughts to give a clear picture of his character — who he is.

There are some people who want a simple view of God and manage to make one up for themselves. I have not got a simple view of God and I cannot preach one, for the more I know, the less I feel I know, and the greatness of God is such that I discover more about him.

I have been trying to give you a picture of God, and we have been going through the alphabet so that you can try and remember something of this teaching. So if someone says to you, "What is God like?" Then you can start, "He is the Almighty and Bountiful Creator" (the "A-B-C"). His divinity and his eternity were the next things that engaged our attention, and then from that — in which he is so different to us — we turn to that in which he is like us; his Fatherly Goodness. Then we looked at the sterner side of his character: his **H**oliness, his **I**ndignation, and his **J**ustice. Then we looked at the softer side of his character: his **K**indness, his **L**ove, and his **M**ercy. Then we considered his **N**ames, of which there are literally hundreds, but we considered some of the most important. Then we considered the **O**rder and the **P**eace, and the **Q**uiet of God, such that before his throne in heaven there is a glassy sea as far as the eye can see. Then we considered his **R**eign and his **S**overeignty — God on the throne.

Now we come to the letters "t" and "u", his **T**riune nature and his **U**nity. This is the point at which we come to something that is so difficult for our minds to take in that some have objected to the idea of believing in the Trinity and said, "My God is simpler than that — that is too complicated." The idea that God is really three persons, and yet at the same time is one, is something that our little mathematical minds cannot comprehend. There are many people who are very good at putting two and two together and making five, but when you tell them three equals one and one equals three then it is beyond them.

There are not only those who have opposed the idea of the Trinity in the name of human reason but those who have opposed it in the name of human religion. Next time a Jehovah's Witness knocks on your door, mention the word "Trinity" to him but shut your door pretty quickly because this is one of those things he cannot abide, nor can that Mormon who knocks the next week. The Christian Scientist and the spiritualist cannot cope with the Trinity either.

But right through the ages every Christian creed has said, "I believe in Father, Son, and Holy Spirit" —three persons, one God, and that is the faith that we believe and teach.

Now I want to turn to the Bible to try and help you understand what we mean by the Trinity and that Unity, not that you may argue with people about it but so that you can say with Saint Patrick: "I bind unto myself today the strong name of the Trinity" —and so that you can begin every morning in life *knowing* Father, Son, and Holy Spirit.

At first glance the Bible seems to be a divided book. We know it is divided into the Old and New Testaments but it might appear to some to be divided on this issue. The Old Testament, they can see, teaches the unity of God, and the New Testament teaches the Trinity. Or, to put it in simple language: the Old Testament says that "God is one" and the New Testament says "God is three." What do we make of this?

Let us look at the Old Testament. You may never have realised what a relief it is to believe in just one God. In the world in which the Old Testament was written there were many gods. Turn to the land of Egypt and you find that they worshipped frogs, flies, bulls and the river Nile. It is interesting that in the time of Moses every one of the ten plagues on Egypt was connected with one of their religions and one of their gods.

Turn to the land of Canaan, and everywhere you looked had Baal or an Asherah. The Baal was the husband god, the Asherah was the wife god. Every little locality had its own husband god and its own wife god with their foul sexual idols—many gods. Turn to the most cultured nation of the ancient world, namely Greece. If you go to the ruins in Greece today you will find that, as Paul said, "I perceive that in many ways you are very superstitious." Read Greek mythology and you will find that they believed in many gods and goddesses.

In many areas of the world even today you may find that people struggle with the anxieties and fears caused by many gods. Missionaries would tell you what a relief it is for people to be told there is only one God. Let me try to help you understand this. Supposing there was a god who looked after our health and a god who looked after our homes and a god who looked after our jobs and another one who looked after our travelling and another who looked after our money and another who looked after the weather and and so on, and you had to try and keep them all happy. What would your prayer life be like?

It is difficult enough with one God to keep it right, but if you had many gods and didn't know who to pray to, and what sort of prayer that particular one liked, you would understand the fears that missionaries meet in such a situation. You might have missed one out, you might have failed to pray to the one that would have done you damage and so invariably with all your altars and your idols you had one altar at the end: "To an unknown god" so that whoever it was that you missed out you could say "Well I did mention you actually, that was to you."

You see the situation? This is not as primitive as you may think. I remember an Irishman showing me a printed list that he had been given of 180 saints to whom he must pray, and opposite each name was the problem he must take to that saint: one whenever he got in his car, another whenever he got a toothache, and the poor man of course was bewildered. To tell him that all he had to do was to go to the one God through Jesus with every problem he had was just wonderful news.

There are some who believe in many gods and there are some religions that believe in only two. A religion in ancient Persia was called Zoroastrianism after its founder, a man named Zoroaster. He taught that there are two gods, one a good god and one a bad one, and that the two are equal in strength and struggling with one another, and your sickness comes from one and your health from the other. Again it was an uncertain situation, so you wondered: "Is that one going to win today, or the other one? Well, that one won yesterday — I wonder if this one will today? You were tossed about between two parts. Into that world came the Jews with a ringing message of hope: "Hear O Israel, the Lord our God, the Lord is one." That was great news for the world.

The Jews still regard it as his greater treasure for the world, a belief in one God. It is right through the Old Testament. Yet it is not enough to believe in one God. That does not save you. Belief in one God is not in itself sufficient. I meet many people who know that I belong to a church and say "Well, I don't want you to think I don't believe in God —I do." They believe in one god — they pick that much up from the Christian faith that has been preached in this land for nearly two thousand years. But more is needed. They believe that there is one god—that's fine, but just a moment, there are other religions that believe in only one. I have lived in Arabia for three years, where the majority religion is Islam. It is significant that this is the only major religion of the world that started after Christ and it came to believe that there is only one deity, but it doesn't save the Muslim.

Furthermore, the New Testament says this: "You believe that God is one," says James, "you do well, even the demons believe that and shudder."

Again, we turn to the New Testament. "Hear O Israel, the Lord our God, the Lord is one" is quoted in both the Old Testament and the New. Now came something that quite shattered those people. As we read through the Gospel accounts a strange thing happens to our faith in God as one. The big question in the Gospels is "Who is Jesus? What is he?" They scratch their heads and they say that he is a man alright, we can see that; he is a real man, a remarkable man, we can see that, too; what manner of man is this that even the winds and waves obey him?

His enemies saw the truth before his friends did, and

his enemies said "Blasphemy, blasphemy." They could see what he was getting at, but it was not until the day of the resurrection (or a week after that) that one of the twelve disciples, the greatest doubter and sceptic of them all, as a Jew used one word to Jesus which was extraordinary. He said "My Lord and my God."

Here is the problem: two persons have now been mentioned, and to distinguish we must give them different names. For if Jesus was God there must be another, for he prayed to him — and he was looking after the world while he was on earth. So we know about God the Father and God the Son. But before Jesus left the disciples, he said that there would be a third person coming: when I return to the Father, I will pray and he will send another to look after you. When you get into Acts you do indeed have yet a third divine person — like the Son in that he teaches and comforts, yet who bears a different name. Now we have the astonishing truth: that God is three.

So Acts tells us that God is three, and throughout the epistles God is three. It is in this familiar text: "The grace of our Lord Jesus Christ, and the love of God, and the fellowship of the Holy Spirit be with you all." Peter, writing to Christians, greets them like this: "Chosen and destined by God the Father and sanctified by the Spirit for obedience to Jesus Christ."

If that were the whole picture it would be comparatively simple. You would either choose to believe the Old Testament and say "God is one" or you would choose to believe the New and say "God is three." Do we have to choose between the two, or could it be that both are right and that both are the truth? The answer is it not only could be true but it is.

Does the Old Testament never say that God is more than one? It does. Earlier in the book I took the names of God, and I gave you the name "God" and I gave you the name

"Lord" and I told you a remarkable fact: of the name "God", two hundred and fifty times it is used in the singular "God", but two thousand times in the Old Testament it is used in the plural: "Gods."

"In the beginning Gods said", or "Gods created". All the way through, in the proportion of eight to one, the name of God is "Gods." Or take the name "Lord." Thirty times in the Old Testament the word "Lord" is in the singular, but three hundred times it is in the plural: "Lords." Let's go back to what Moses said to Israel: "Hear O Israel, the Lord our Gods, the Lord is one." Even while he told them God was one, he told them he was more than one. Amazing, and the Jews to this day have a veil over their faces, they can't see it.

They can read the Old Testament: "And God said 'Let *us* make man in *our* own image'," and they still cannot see it in their own scriptures. God said in Genesis 3, "Behold man has become like one of *us*," and still they cannot see it. Even that word "one" is interesting. There are two words for "one" in the Hebrew language and one means a single thing by itself and the other always is what we call a "compound word" meaning more than one. Does the Old Testament ever say that there are three? Yes, here is the prophet Isaiah describing the Messiah who is to come, and he is actually putting words into the mouth of the Messiah by inspiration, and this is what he says: "And now the Lord God has sent me and his Spirit" —and still the Jews read it and they cannot see. So though it is true that the Old Testament speaks of the unity of God, hidden within it for anyone with eyes to see there is the Trinity. Now see what I have done. I have said that the New Testament teaches that God is three, but when I look closely again at the New Testament I find that it too teaches that God is one. There came a scribe one day to Jesus and said, "What is the greatest commandment?" and Jesus said, "Hear O Israel, the Lord our God, the Lord is one and you shall love the Lord your God with all your heart and soul and mind and strength." The scribe said, "You have spoken well Teacher. You have truly said that he is one and there is no other but he," and Jesus didn't quarrel with him.

Listen to Matthew 28, where Jesus says to the disciples "Go into all the world, baptising them into the name..." not the *names*, the *name* "of the Father and of the Son and of the Holy Spirit" —one name. Think of Paul speaking of meat offered to idols in 1 Corinthians 8 where he says that there is one God.

Now come into the Holy of Holies, into John 17, into our Lord's own prayer life, and see him there on the night before he died, praying. He prays: "I want my disciples to be one. I want them to be united.... That they all may be one even *as we are one*." All through the prayer you have the "us" of Genesis 1 all over again — "us", "we". This is Jesus Christ talking to his Father.

Incidentally, John 17 is often used now to press us all into church unity, but *the unity that Christ prayed for is the sort of unity he had with the Father.* It is a unity of thoughts so that both think alike; it is a unity of words so that both say the same thing; it is a unity of deed — not that they do the identical thing, but what one does is complementary to what the other does. It is above all a unity of nature and Spirit, and any attempt to create an artificial unity that is not that sort of unity is a terrible substitute for the real thing. Jesus also prayed that they may be *in us*.

Now we have seen it, haven't we? The Old Testament emphasises his unity but does not exclude his Trinity. The New Testament emphasises his Trinity but does not exclude his unity. Put it together and I am lost in wonder, love and praise, and I just have to say: God, you are three and you are one, and I don't understand it, and I can't explain it, but I know it is true, and I know that is my faith and I bind to myself today the strong name of the Trinity.

Finally, there are three ways in which you could come to believe in the Trinity. Possibly by way of *explanation*, but I doubt that. It is beyond me to explain. I have heard people say it is like the root and the trunk and the branches of a tree, but that doesn't explain it because that is still one tree, not three trees in one. Some have said it's "like having a body, a mind, and a spirit; that's three in one", but it isn't — that would still be only one person, not three persons in one.

The nearest I could get to it would be to talk of marriage, for in Genesis 2 it says that a man shall leave his father and mother and cleave to his wife, and they shall become one flesh. The word "one" there is a compound word and it is the same word used of God in one — two people who become one flesh, that's two becoming one. Can you add a third and begin to see that three in one is how God is?

You could come to it through *explanation* but I doubt that is likely. You might come to believe it because of *exposition*. I have tried to expound the Word of God to you and show you that it is there, and that may have convinced you, perhaps more than you have been convinced before, that this is your God. But there is a third way, and it is the way the apostles came, and it is the way that will ultimately make this your faith —it is the way of experience.

How do you come to Trinitarian believing by way of experience? Did you notice the order in which the Trinity is mentioned in the "grace"? The first person of the Trinity is not mentioned first, the second is mentioned first: "The grace of our Lord Jesus...." Many people believe in one God, but one day, by the *grace* of God we come to the point where we realise that Jesus came to save us. Though we were utterly abhorrent to God, to share love and mercy Jesus came and found us; Jesus died on the cross for me and went through a foul criminal's death to save me for eternal life.

When you come to the *grace* of the Lord Jesus, you say, "Only God could have done that," and you have found the *second* person. Then you begin to wonder: who sent Jesus? Why did it all happen? Who thought of it? Who planned it? You begin to discover the *love of God*. You don't come to the love of God first, you come to the grace of God first, and through that you come to the Father and find the love of God, and you have found the *first* person.

Then you discover that you are not the only one that this has happened to, and you discover that there are other people who have found the *grace* of Jesus Christ and the *love* of God, and you find that you have been born again, and born into a family, and you find that as you meet with them the Holy Spirit becomes real in your experience, and you have found the third person. Yet you know, even though you have found three persons, they are so one that you can hardly tell them apart, and you hardly know who you are praying to sometimes. The Holy Spirit seems the Spirit of God, and the Spirit of Christ, and you are just caught up in him, you have experienced the Trinity, and you can now say he is yours.

One final comment. It has helped me to distinguish between his "threeness" and his "oneness". He is three *persons*, not one person. Each has his own centre of consciousness, knowing that he is neither of the other two. So they can converse with each other and obviously do. But they share *one nature*, thinking, feeling, acting and reacting in the same way. They work together in perfect co-operation for our creation and redemption, each making his own contribution. Even Satan could not divide them, though he tried hard enough.

Praise God the holy trinity!

9

VENGEANCE; WRATH

As we begin this study, I do ask you first to read Romans chapter 1. It helps our understanding as we look at this aspect of God's character. Romans 1 is a very serious passage, but it is the beginning of the gospel. Canon Max Warren wrote a book about the meaning of the cross, and his first chapter was entitled *The Good News of God's Wrath*. That is an amazing heading, but it is right — God's wrath is the beginning of the gospel.

In Romans 12:19 we have these words: "Beloved, never avenge yourselves but leave it to the wrath of God for it is written, 'Vengeance is mine. I will repay, says the Lord.'" If anybody wants to know what the practical outcome will be of studying this aspect of the character of God, it is this: you will never try to take personal revenge on anyone for whatever they do to you; you will learn to leave God to repay them — and that is a tremendous lesson to learn.

But there are other deep lessons concerned with our own persons, not only with our relationships with others. It is absolutely vital that we should not only come to terms with this truth, but find the way of escape from it. John Bunyan, writing that famous book *The Pilgrim's Progress*, began the story with a man who was handed a piece of parchment on which was written just these words, "Flee from the wrath to come."

That was what began that man's search for the heavenly city. One of the difficulties today is that because this truth is not being taught properly, Christians are beginning the Christian life without reading that piece of parchment, and the result is what I would call "mini-Christians" who don't have a big enough gratitude to God for all that he has saved them from, and therefore they don't love him much because they do not realise how much they have been forgiven. Now both the words "vengeance" and "wrath" are going right out of fashion.

Let me take first the word "vengeance" or its modern English equivalent "retribution". It is very interesting that in all the discussion which took place in the twentieth century concerning prison reform, and particularly in the debate and discussion about capital punishment, the argument did not centre on this idea as it should have done. There are three reasons for which someone may be judicially punished. One is reformation—you hope by punishing him he will turn over a new leaf and not do it again. The second is deterrence—when you hope that because there is a possibility of being punished, a potential offender won't commit the crime. The third is retribution—that someone has done wrong and so deserves to suffer.

Of course, capital punishment cannot possibly reform a person—execute someone and you can't do anything with them after that. I would personally feel that there was no deterrence in capital punishment. The figures showed that countries in Europe that did not have capital punishment had about the same number of murders as those which did. The real issue when we discussed capital punishment was retribution, but the arguments put forward carefully evaded that principle.

The big question is this: is vengeance or retribution a right or a wrong thing? That should be the basis from which we approach the subject. Now what about the word "wrath"? In these days wrath is considered a weakness of character and in the days of chatty, calm television discussions, a man who shows deep passion is considered suspect, even neurotic, a social misfit. So when we read the word "wrath" we instinctively say, "Well that is not the normal, mature character's reaction." A mature person keeps calm, cool and collected.

So are vengeance and wrath wrong in themselves? Or do we only consider them wrong because we are quite incapable of exercising them rightly? Let me say straightaway that vengeance and wrath in human beings are usually wrong, because we are quite incapable of either and still maintaining self-control. If we take our revenge, we lose our temper. Therefore the Bible says, "Never avenge yourselves." You are not safe to do so. Never get your own back, never hit the other chap who has hit you, because you are not safe to do so—never. That is a strong command.

The Bible also says that you should never go to bed with wrath in your heart, "Never let the sun go down on your wrath." If you are angry with someone, get it sorted out before you go to bed or you will have a bad night because you have got a bad conscience. It also says, "The wrath of man worketh not the righteousness of God." Therefore we are told that we are to forgive our brothers seventy times seven, to turn the other cheek if he hits one, and not to apply the rule "an eye for an eye and a tooth for a tooth" to our personal relations.

But because vengeance and wrath are wrong in a human being they are not wrong in a *holy* being—that is what the Bible is telling us. The only One in the universe who is safe enough to exercise either is the holy God. When we turn to study God, we find that he tells us not to get our own back, but we are to leave it to him. If your enemy is hungry, feed him. If he thirsts, give him a drink. God can repay all that he has done to you

When other nations were grinding the Jews into the dust, God's message was: I will bring my vengeance. Cheer up. I'll repay, you don't need to try. I'll deal with these people.

That is why whenever we are tempted to hit someone back and pay back evil for evil we should leave it to God. *In other words, here is something that we are told not to do that God actually does, which is extraordinary.*

Our attitude to our enemies must not be the attitude of God to our enemies. In other words, we can't be trusted to take vengeance. God can, and he will. Why? *Because God is in perfect control of himself, and his vengeance and wrath will be absolutely just and fair.*

Shall I give you one example of how unjust we become? When we are angry with someone we usually take it out on someone else, don't we? All right, you have fallen out with your boss at work and you are terribly angry with him — there is wrath in your heart. Who gets the brunt of it? Your wife, when you get home, perhaps? Is that fair? Is that just? So often our vengeance goes further than what we received from the person or it hurts someone else.

Lamech: "I've slayed a man for hitting me. I killed him for just bruising me." Our vengeance tends to get out of control very quickly, but God's vengeance never does. Now as soon as I say that God is a God of vengeance and wrath some people have a sense of awful disappointment and even dismay and say, "But this isn't the Christian God, is it?" A man called Marcion said many centuries ago: "That's the Old Testament God." So he said: "Christians shouldn't study the Old Testament, it's too full of vengeance and wrath." So he cut out the Old Testament. He soon found when he studied his New Testament he had to cut out a lot of that too. He had to cut out the book of Revelation for a start. But then he found he had to cut out even parts of John's Gospel, and by the time he had finished he had precious little left. Now Marcion was not the last person to do that kind of thing. You may not do it with a pair of scissors. You can do it mentally by just not reading certain parts of the Bible, but there is not enough left for a *magnified* view of God, a big enough view of God.

Why then do we react against these two truths? It may be due to our human ideas of wrath but I would think it was also due to our human ideas of love, which have no room for this in them, and that is the fault of our inadequate conception of love. When I preach about the love of God I invariably put an adjective in front of the word "love" deliberately, so that you don't get the idea that when I say "love" I'm speaking of human love magnified. I usually put the adjective "holy" in front. *God's love is a holy love.*

Since there are very few holy people on earth, you will not get your idea of God's love from human love. You must take your ideas of human love from God's love. That would be the better way around. The final test for all our ideas of God is whether Jesus was like this. I agree entirely with those who say that they will not accept something in the Old Testament that is incompatible with Jesus. I personally have found that everything in the Old Testament is compatible with Jesus; that is why I accept it. I would not believe that God was a God of vengeance and wrath unless Jesus was a person like that.

As the little schoolboy said, "God is Jesus everywhere." I don't know what the theologians would make of that, but it is a terrific description. God is Jesus everywhere, so what was Jesus like in relation to these two things? Well, first look at what he said. I take it you would agree with me that the parables of Jesus about the kingdom of God tell us what God is like — that whether it is the father with his two sons or the owner of the vineyard, he is speaking about God.

Let me take at random two parables. Consider first the Parable of the Wedding Feast. Do you know what happened when people refused to come to the wedding feast? The king was angry and sent troops to destroy men and city. Matthew 22—that is the teaching of Jesus. Another parable is the Parable of the Unforgiving Servant. In his anger the master handed him over to tormentors till all was paid.

Now you may say, "Well those are details in a story and you can't press every detail of the story." But Jesus said that anyone who believes in the Son [Jesus] has eternal life, but ... anyone who refuses to believe in the Son shall not see life: the wrath of God rests on him" (see John 3:33ff). The whole of John's Gospel is the gospel. You can't pick and choose.

But what about Jesus in his actions —did he show wrath in his actions? He wasn't very often angry. That made him different from us, but when he was, he was. There are only five occasions recorded in the Gospels in which Jesus was angry. One was when a man with a withered hand was healed in the synagogue one Sabbath. The leaders were angry because that happened and was disturbing to their ideas and their service. Jesus looked around on them with anger. Oh he was angry! They said that it was working on Sabbath.

Another time, Jesus went to the temple, which was to be a house of prayer, and there was one part of the temple reserved for the outsider, the Gentile. Because God's house was to be a house of prayer for all nations, anybody could come to it, so there was a courtyard for the Gentiles. When Jesus came in, it was full of people buying and selling animals and changing money so that they could get the temple currency to pay the temple tax. It was just a commercialised bazaar and nobody could have prayed at all in that atmosphere.

Because they had filled the court of the Gentiles with this, no outsider could get into that place to pray, because they couldn't go into the quiet part; they kept that for the Jewish priests. When Jesus saw this he was terribly angry. He got a whip and he whipped men out of that temple—that's Jesus. No gentle Jesus meek and mild there. He didn't whip the animals, he whipped the men. He turned over their tables of money changing and he said: Get out! This is my Father's house.

To apply that personally today, whenever there is a church where outsiders feel they cannot come and pray with the people of God, I am quite sure the Lord Jesus is angry. He meant us to be a church wide open to everybody so that they could come and feel, "I have a place to pray here."

That is Jesus' anger. So I would say that anger which was shown later by his cursing of a fig tree, and the fig tree dying, is the wrath of God showing in Jesus Christ.

We turn to another question: what makes God angry? Why does his wrath come upon men? According to my reading of the New Testament there are only two things that make God angry, and you can relate everything else to these two. On the one hand is *immorality*, and on the other hand is *idolatry* —or, to put it in other words, there are those who treat themselves and their fellow human beings in a wrong way, and those who treat God in a wrong way. God meant us and made us to love him with all our heart and soul and mind and strength, and he made us to love our neighbours as ourselves. Whenever we do something that worships a creature instead of the Creator, that is what the Bible means by idolatry. You don't need a little god of wood or stone in your heart. You just need possessions that you worship and live for.

Covetousness is idolatry according to the New Testament and for immorality, you don't need to have done the kind of thing that gets into the Sunday papers. You just need to have been a gossip. That is listed in Romans 1 under immorality because you are breaking your love for your neighbour by being a gossip about them, and it is these two things that make God angry. No wonder that Paul says in one of his letters: "By nature we are all children of wrath" — because you and I have done things that have broken both those relationships and richly deserve God's anger.

The next question is: how does God show he is angry? As you get to know me, you find out when I am angry. You may see me shake, or you may find me spluttering and my words become uncontrolled. You know when a person is angry. You can tell. How can you tell when God is angry? How does it show? You can't look at his face; you can't see him. You can't hear spluttering words; you can't hear him.

The Bible distinguishes between how God shows his anger *today* and how he will show it in *the day of his wrath*. Let me first of all deal with how he shows his anger now. He does it by doing two things: by *removing inward restraints* from people and *imposing outward restraints* upon them. This is a process which reveals God's wrath upon a human society.

I do believe that Britain is revealing both of these trends at this very moment. If you want to check up, read Romans 1 again, then look at the national and international news.

When men give God up, God gives them up to themselves. He stops speaking to them through their conscience; he stops holding them back. He says: all right, do what you want to do if you don't want me to help you to live a good life, then I'll let you live the kind of life that you really would without my help to show you just what kind of a person you are. I'll take the restraints off, I'll remove the voice of conscience. You just do whatever you wish. You find that their minds then get perverted and they can't think straight, they cannot accept the truth. They deliberately try and misunderstand. Have you ever tried to convince someone of the truth of God who is living like this? They cannot understand. It seems that even if you answer their questions they have still got more and they have no will to understand. Their mind is darkened and God has let their mind go because they thought they could think without him. Their bodies become perverted and even the relationship between male and female goes wrong, and male with male do unspeakable things.

Now this is our society; this is what is happening around us. If God only showed his anger that way, society would really go to pieces, but I also pointed out that *his anger today will be shown in imposing outward restraints*. In other words, God is saying: I remove the inward ones. You can do what you like but instead of stopping you inwardly I'll stop you outwardly. You need to read Romans 13 — the police are described in the Bible as God's instrument of his wrath to restrain the evildoer. But instead of the police becoming the friend of the public, they will become the enemy of the public in this context.

Now is this not relevant to what you are reading in the press? Is this not relevant to how police officers are feeling today? Is this not relevant to the whole social set up in which we live? God is saying, "I remove the inward restraints but I'm still going to control you, but I'll have to control you from the outside." I think it may not be long before more police in this country have to be armed, as some already are. Britain giving God up must face the penalty of having God give Britain up. This is his anger. It shows in the news media.

We are a nation that has a church and chapel within reach of everybody in this land. We are a nation that has had the gospel for nearly two thousand years. It was brought to us by the Roman soldiers originally, and the first Christian martyr in this land was St Alban, a Roman soldier after whom a town was named. We have had the Bible in our own tongue. We have multitudes of translations of the Word of God.

Yet I would guess that less than two percent in this country really know Jesus Christ as Saviour and Lord. That is about the number you will find that really can tell you "I believe." I know that more turn up at Christmas and Easter. I know that most still have a minister to bury or cremate them. What does that mean? The question is: have we given God up from Monday to Saturday as well as Sunday?

Now to the future. From what I have told you, you must be aware now that God is angry with our nation but the world doesn't realise it. There is coming a day when the world will see that God is angry. It is connected with the second visit of Christ to this world. When they see him, they will see a face almost identical with the face that the Jewish money changers saw that day in the temple.

Let me give you largely Christ's own words for this because it is so serious that I would not dare to give you what I thought. One day God's anger is going to burst upon this world. It is described vividly in the book of Revelation. Have you noticed how many people refuse to read that book and say, "You can't understand it"? Have you noticed that people almost try to misunderstand it, and therefore dismiss it, because it is the one book that tells us this. Under the pictures of seven seals and seven trumpets and seven bowls, described as bowls of wrath, we have a very clear picture of that day. Who said that book is obscure? In simple, straightforward language, Revelation describes what is coming. It describes the way those left alive after tremendous turbulence still refused to worship God. They would not renounce their demon worship nor their idols made of gold and silver, brass, stone, and wood, which neither see nor hear nor walk. Neither did they change their mind and attitude about all their murders and witchcraft, their immorality, and their theft. Such is the human heart—it still does not learn the lesson.

Finally, the seven bowls of the wrath of God are emptied

out upon the earth.Then we have a description of a sea that congeals, springs that are contaminated, sun that burns too much, total darkness following, the last world war, and lightning, thunder, and hail, and then the end of the world and the collapse of civilisation. Everybody will know that God is angry in those days and then it will all be over. Then God is going to make a new heaven and a new earth, which will be good.

Is this true? It is. It is this present world we see around us which is the world of fantasy. This is the escapist world, running away from this fact. How can I prove to you that these things are going to happen? Well, we have God's Word for it, but if that is not enough there is enough proof in history to tell you that God's wrath is real and must some day catch up. God does not send his bill in every Friday, but one day we will pay.

How do I prove it from history? I could tell you the account of Noah, and about Sodom and Gomorrah but you know about it. I could tell you the story of the people of Israel themselves. Why did only two men out of two and a half million people get into the promised land? The answer is that God said: "I swore in my wrath that they should not enter into my rest." I could mention Jericho and Babylon, Nineveh, Tyre and Jerusalem itself. I could remind you of the words of Jesus in the last week of his earthly ministry that Jerusalem would know the days of the vengeance of God. He said, "Woe to women expecting children at that time. Woe to those with little babies." It was going to be a terrible day, and the day came in AD 70. I could go through history and point to nation after nation whose leaders set themselves up as gods and defied God. I could point to the ends of those men and nations.

I stood just outside the ruins of a bunker in Berlin, knowing that there the body of the man who for twenty years plunged the world into suffering was burned with petrol. He said his kingdom, his reich, would last for a thousand years. History is full of the wrath of God, but the one proof I am going to bring to you is amazingly enough the one proof of God's mercy, and the place where you can find a way out of all this, and a way that will prepare you for the great day that is coming: the cross of Jesus Christ.

If somebody wants proof of the wrath of God, then I say, "Why did God do that to Jesus?" You will notice throughout the book of Revelation that the wrath of God is always pictured as a cup of wine to be drunk. "He is trampling out the vintage where the grapes of wrath are stored," and the cup will be given to men to drink. Why do you think Jesus prayed with drops of blood streaming from his brow, "If it be possible, take this cup from me"? It wasn't just physical death. What was this cup that he shrank from drinking? It was the cup of the wrath of God. The anger of God against sin was going to be focused. Does the book of Revelation say that one day the sun will go out and we shall have to live in total darkness to tell us that God is angry? When Jesus died the sun went out and there was total darkness. It was not an eclipse because in fact it was the time of the full moon, the Passover, and there is no eclipse at full moon and an eclipse doesn't last three hours. The sun went out because God was angry. Why should God be angry with the only perfect life that was ever lived? He wasn't angry with that life, but here is the meaning of the cross: "God made him to be sin who knew no sin." As it were, he drew all the anger of God into himself, and died saying, "My God, my God, why have you forsaken me?" He went through hell. Why? I'll tell you, in the words of Paul in Romans: "Being now justified by his blood, we shall be saved from the wrath of God through him." That is why. The wrath of God was directed on Christ that we might never face it—that is the gospel of Jesus Christ.

It is offensive to those who are modern in their thinking. It is offensive to those who don't believe the Bible is the Word of God. But those who believe it, who like Bunyan's pilgrim take that parchment and read "Flee from the wrath to come", and then say, "Tell me how to flee", and who ultimately come, as that pilgrim did, to a hill with a cross on it, who climb that hill looking at the cross, find as they do so that the burden of their guilt tumbles from off their back and rolls down the hill and falls into a sepulchre, and you can see it no more. They go on walking to the heavenly city — they know the answer.

We have been saved from the wrath of God by the blood of Jesus Christ. I could put it no more simply than that: all the anger and the vengeance that I justly deserve, Jesus took for me. Nothing could be simpler, and when you believe that, then you can look forward to passing right through that day that is coming — into a new heaven and a new earth, which will be utterly good, and so will you.

10

X; YEAR; ZEAL

We need to remember that most of us in most congregations are Gentiles. It is only of God's goodness that we ever heard of Jesus, but from the very beginning God called Jew and Gentile. The shepherds were Jews, the wise men were Gentiles, but they met at the nativity, and Jew and Gentile come together at this point. The tragedy is that, by and large, the Jews do not see it and are still waiting. I said in the 1960s that it is the Gentiles who have to go to the Jews and say: "Don't you know? Have you not heard? The Messiah has come." But in the past half century Messianic Jewish congregations have been growing in many countries. One day the Jews will know, as a nation, and that will be a most thrilling day.

X, Y and Z are the three letters left now. They are actually the easiest. We took V and W, the vengeance and wrath of God, and Christians think of the second coming of Christ to judge the quick and the dead. They think of the day of God's vengeance and the day of Christ's wrath that is coming. Now, therefore, the most fundamental question must be: "How can I prepare for that day?" The answer is: x, y, z. Here is my text and I don't think any of the three letters occur in it: "For God was pleased to have all his fulness dwell in him [the Son], and through him to reconcile to himself all things, whether things on earth or things in heaven, by making peace through his blood, shed on the cross" (Colossians 1:19–20).

The letter "**X**", in modern English, stands for that which you don't know and that which you do know. For example, in algebra the first thing you learn is that the letter "x" stands for the figure you don't know. It is the unknown quantity, figure or factor. But if you look on a map and you see an "x" on it, that tells you that somebody knows something about that spot — it is likely to be the place where you will find what you want, maybe the place where treasure is found. To many people, God is the *unknown*. He is the great "x", the great God who they just don't know. A student once asked me after a talk I gave in a college: "You keep using the word "God" — what does that word mean?" What is God? God was "x" to that person, the unknown. Yet for Christians "x" marks the very spot where the unknown God becomes a God you can know most intimately.

You know of course that the New Testament was written in the Greek language. The Greek initial letter for the word "Christ" (*Christos*) looks rather like an "X" in English but is pronounced more like *chi*. So, at an early stage, this letter was beginning to mean a very great deal to the early Christians, and it meant one thing: the actual letter, the beginning of Christ.

Now one of the early Christian symbols was a fish. If you had seen a fish drawn on a wall hurriedly you would have known a Christian had been around. It was a secret sign between Christians when they could not openly acknowledge one another. They would meet, and one would just trace a very simple outline with his stick in the dust and put an "eye" in it and they would know that they were Christians. Why did they use that symbol? What's a fish got to do with it? I know some of the disciples were fishermen, but a fish was used because the Greek word for fish was *ichthus*. (The "ch" being a transliteration of Greek "chi", looking a bit like our "X"). Hanging a word on each of the Greek letters for the word "fish", they came up with a most amazing thing. They hung the word *yesus* (Jesus) on the first letter, in Greek the "i", and that, together with the rest of the letters that mean "fish" stand for: "Jesus Christ, Son of God, Saviour." In this very neat way they would take the symbol of the fish and tell each other: I believe what you believe but I dare not say so openly; I will just draw a fish and you will know I believe in Jesus Christ, the Son of God, our Saviour.

That is a wonderful creed and it is all in the "fish". As a kind of shorthand of the name of Christ they would take the first two letters and take an "x" and what looks to us like a "p" which is actually their "r", and use that as their symbol.

So we now know what the "X" meant to the early Christians. It didn't just mean the unknown or the known, it meant Christ. That is why to this very day you might write "Christmas" in shorthand as "Xmas". I want to say x marks the spot where God revealed himself in Christ, and where treasure may be found. Though the wise men brought their treasures, in fact they were looking for treasure and they found it at Bethlehem.

What is it about Christ that makes him so important to Christians? Why do we talk about our religion as *Christ*-ianity. Why do we call ourselves *Christ*ians? Because there are two facts about Christ which make him the most important person in the whole of history.

As John says, if somebody wrote down everything about Christ that could be written, the world itself could not contain the books. The greater a man, the more books you can write about him. But there are two basic facts about Christ that you need to know, to begin to believe. First, in his life he brought God to man. Second, in his death he brought man to God. Here are the two basic sides of what he set out to do, and he did it. In Christ, God is brought to man in his life, and that life is continued from the resurrection as we know; and in his death he brought men to God.

I once heard an agnostic say, "I cannot believe that God is a person if he has no body." This man was saying that he could not think of a *person* without a body. So he could not believe that God is a "he", although he might believe that God is an "it". To many people the word "God" really just means "it" — some*thing*, some power behind the universe, but to say "he" means a person. This agnostic said: "I just can't see that; If God had a body like mine I could believe that he was a person" — which raises the question: could you ever get God inside a human body? Could you ever take the God of the whole universe and get him down to that size?

There are three answers people have given to this. There is a group who say that God can be found in *no-one*. You could never find a God who could be small enough to get into a man and therefore you never will find this. A second group say that you can find God in every man. I have met people who believe this, and teach that in fact if you look within yourself you will find God because God is in *everyone*. But you finish up with a very similar feeling to looking down a well and seeing your own reflection. You finish up with your own religious feelings. You don't find God that way.

God is not to be found in *no-one* and he is not to be found in *everyone*. The Christian faith is found in *one* man, called Jesus Christ. Now you notice what the text says—that the whole of God, everything of God, or as the Bible puts it, the fullness of the godhead actually dwelt in Jesus bodily.

For the first time, God was really *knowable*. Before that, men and women had a sense that God was difficult to get through to. So how do you get through to him? But God was contracted to a span. I could say it even more boldly that God became about one foot long when the babe of Bethlehem was born. Now think of that — when Mary looked down at the cradle and saw that baby about that long, the fullness of the godhead was dwelling bodily in him.

This is so amazing that if I were not a Christian I couldn't believe it. Twelve disciples who lived with him for three years couldn't believe it either. He told them time and time again who he was, but they didn't get the message until one day when it dawned on them. Shortly before Jesus died, one of the disciples, Philip, said to him, "If you let us see God once we will believe all you say about him." Jesus said (and I paraphrase): "Oh Philip, how long must I be with you? I have been with you for three years, have you not seen God yet? Don't you realise that if you look at me you're looking at God? Don't you realise that if you see me, you've seen my Father?" Philip didn't realise it, but just a few days later, one of the other disciples, the most sceptical of the whole lot, would say to Jesus, "My Lord and my God!" He saw that Jesus is God in a human body — God we can get to know.

The minds of many people cannot cope with an everlasting God and so they ask the silly question "who made God" because they find it hard to understand the idea that he never did need to be made; that he has always been there. But God came in Christ so we begin to see what he is like. God is within reach not only of our hands but of our minds. We can not only touch him, we can understand something about him. This is the most glorious thing, and therefore for the Christian "X" marks the spot where God may be found in Jesus Christ, and I would say to people: you never will know God until you know Jesus.

You will never know him to talk to until you have talked to Jesus. You will never understand how kind God is until you have tasted the kindness of Jesus. You will never know the mercy of God until you have found it in Jesus Christ. All that I have explained so far, right through from the letter

119

"A" to the letter "W", you will find in Jesus Christ. Did God create the world? —so did Jesus. Jesus made the mountains and the oceans. Jesus made the tree on which they ultimately hung him. Jesus made the countryside. Jesus made the leaves and the sky and the clouds. Jesus made it all. Without him was not anything made that was made.

Is God eternal? So is Jesus. Is God fatherly? That's because Jesus is his Son and reveals the fatherhood of God. Is God good? So is Jesus. Is God holy? So is Jesus. Is God indignant over sins? So is Jesus. Is God just? So is Jesus. Is God kind and loving and merciful? So is Jesus.

What is the name of God? Is it "Jehovah"? No, I showed you how Jesus has replaced that name. The order and peace and quiet may be seen in Jesus as he sleeps in a boat in the middle of a storm. The reign and sovereignty of God may be seen in the fact that Jesus is now on the throne, and all his enemies will become his footstool, and all authority in heaven and earth has been given to him. The Trinity and the unity only makes sense through Jesus. The vengeance and wrath of God will be seen in Jesus when he comes again— x marks the spot.

Isaiah wrote: "Behold a virgin shall conceive and bear a son and his name shall be called Emmanuel, which means 'God with us'" (see Isaiah 7:14). Then in chapter nine: "For to us a child is born, to us a son is given, and the government will be upon his shoulder and his name will be called wonderful, counsellor, mighty God...." Do you know what the next verse says? *"The zeal of the Lord shall perform this."* There is my letter "**Z**".

The Roman forces occupied the Holy Land and they were so powerful that people generally gave into them and accepted this enemy occupation, but there was a resistance movement of Jewish terrorists who repeatedly tried to throw the Romans out. They were called "Zealots". We are told in the scriptures to maintain our spiritual zeal. What does this word "zeal" mean? Zeal can be seen in countless missionaries, and in many Christian reformers who have changed conditions for the poor and suffering.

Zeal is seeing a situation that is wrong and doing something about it. God did something about this world of sinners, sending Jesus his Son. The zeal of the Lord performed it and so we've got our letter "X" and our letter "Z", but there is something more. If you are ever going to restore a broken relationship you must do two things. You must bring the two parties together, but that will be no use unless you then reconcile the difference between them. In a broken marriage it is no use just saying, "All right both come to my house next Thursday evening, and then put them into a room and shut the door and lock them in and say I won't let you out until you agree." That might work in a few cases but I very much doubt it would work in many. What you must do, having brought them together, is to work to remove the difference — to *reconcile* the two.

Christians have taken as a symbol of their faith an X that stands on end. It's still an X and it still marks the spot but it's something much deeper: the cross. Has it ever struck you that Christians are quite extraordinary in having as the symbol of their faith an instrument of execution and torture? What would you think if standing on a communion table, for example, there was a little model of a hangman's rope, a gallows, and we had that at the centre of our faith? What would you think if there was a lovely little model of an electric chair or a gas chamber there, or a block with an axe lying beside it? What would you really think? You would think: these people are morbid. But alas, because we have become so familiar with the cross, the horror of it escapes us. But that's what the cross is—it's a horrible thing. It's only because we have never seen it actually that we dare to use it as an ornament and think it is attractive on a chain or a bracelet or necklace. Why should Christians make so much of such a horrible thing? It's not because of its shape. Many people seem to think the shape of the cross is all you need, so they will shape it in stone or metal or wood. The shape of the cross doesn't save you. Some people think it is the wood of the cross that helps you, and this is the origin of the saying "touch wood". I hope you never say that because it is a denial of your faith. Sometimes I say to somebody, "How are you today?" "Well I'm very well—touch wood." Why touch wood? It goes back to the Middle Ages, touching the cross. It is sheer superstition. The wood of the cross doesn't save. What is it about the cross that does save, then? "For in Christ all the fullness of God was pleased to dwell," [X marks the spot] "and through him to reconcile to himself all things, whether on earth or in heaven, making peace by the blood of his cross" — X marks the spot. In other words, it is not the shape of the cross, it is not the wood of the cross, it is the *blood* of the cross.

This is one of the most offensive things about Christianity and yet it is the secret. It is the blood of Jesus Christ that saves people. People don't like this idea, they are offended by it. But without the shedding of blood, that barrier between God and mankind could never have been dealt with.

On a hill outside a city wall where the cross marks the spot — Jesus saved us by the blood of his cross. I can't understand that but I know it is true. I know that one day, many centuries earlier, families stayed in their homes late one night and they heard wailing coming up the street as in each house a baby died. Maybe it was a young man but it was the firstborn in every house. Can you imagine what it was like to hear the wails start at the bottom of your road and hear them coming nearer and nearer? Then to hear them next door, somebody's died next door, and you wait in silence, and then the wailing starts next door, on the other side, and then the next door, and you know that death has passed over you—how? What did you do? How did you prevent that coming to your house? You did one thing: you took some blood of a lamb and you painted your doorpost with it.

Now the colour of blood is the hardest colour to see at midnight, but it wasn't man who was looking at it, it was God. When God saw that blood of Jesus, he passed over. This is the heart of our faith, that's why the cross marks the spot. That's why X becomes for us a most precious symbol, standing upright in the earth. It was at that spot that this amazing thing happened and we were made right with God. Jesus died on the cross that he might bring the the unjust to the just, the sinner to the righteous, the bad man to the good God, and to reconcile us all in himself through the blood of the cross.

What about the letter "Y"? I traced the cross to its origin, its cause: the zeal of the Lord. I now look forward to its effect and I now bring in another phrase, which Jesus used in his preaching. He said, "The Spirit of the Lord is upon me because he has anointed me to preach good news to the poor. He sent me to proclaim release to the captives, recovering of sight to the blind, and to set at liberty those that are bruised and to proclaim" [what?] "... the acceptable year of the Lord", and here is my other letter. The acceptable year means the year in which God will accept. We are still in the time when God will accept people for the sake of Jesus Christ. Pray God that more people will come to know him, looking at Jesus on the cross and saying: "That man was God dying for my sins."

I ask you now to look back to the day of your *anno domini*. I don't mean how old you are physically. I'll tell you my *anno domini*. It was 1947. That was the year of the Lord for me. That is the year in which God's zeal sending Christ to be born and to die for me, came through to JDP and made sense, that was my *anno domini*. That was the year in which the Lord accepted me for his sake. I pray that you will come to know the year of the Lord if you don't already. The zeal of the Lord did this. He was so desperate to help you and to save you, so urgently did he want to do something about the state of the world that he sent Christ and "X" marks the spot where God became man and was brought to us. But you must take the x of xmas and you must turn it the right way up till it becomes another place, a hill outside a city wall, and that marks the spot where *anno domini* begins for you, the *year* of the Lord in which he accepts you.

CPSIA information can be obtained at www.ICGtesting.com
Printed in the USA
LVOW10s2257121214

418589LV00001B/1/P